THE ILLUSTRATED

BHAGAVAD GITA

THE ILLUSTRATED

BHAGAVAD GITA

A NEW TRANSLATION

with COMMENTARY *by*

Ranchor Prime

BARRON'S

First edition for the United States and Canada
published in 2003 by Barron's Educational Series, Inc.

First published in 2003 under the title *The Illustrated Bhagavad Gita*
by Godsfield Press, Laurel House, Station Approach, Alresford, Hants,
SO24 9JH, United Kingdom.

Text © Copyright by Ranchor Prime
Book © Copyright by Godsfield Press

The right of Ranchor Prime to be identified as the author of this work
has been asserted by him in accordance with the
UK Copyright, Designs and Patents Act of 1988.

Designed and created by The Bridgewater Book Company

All inquiries should be addressed to:
Barron's Educational Series, Inc.
250 Wireless Boulevard
Hauppauge, New York 11788

http://www.barronseduc.com

International Standard Book Number 0–7641–2223–1
Library of Congress Catalog Card Number 2001097846

Printed in China
9 8 7 6 5 4 3 2 1

Dedication
For my teacher, Srila A.C.Bhaktivedanta Swami Prabhupada, who
introduced me to Krishna, and my children Rupi and Anasuya, whose
questions inspired this book.

Acknowledgments
My good friend Ian Roberts encouraged me to write this book and
overcame all my protestations; my elder godbrother Jayadvaita
Swami gave freely his advice; Martin Palmer showed the way by his
example; and Debbie Thorpe had the imagination and understanding
to lend her timely support. I am grateful to them all, and to my
editors Mark Truman, Lizzy Gray, and Sarah Doughty. My special
thanks are for Lena, who patiently listened.

Contents

Introduction

O Krishna, tell me again of your mystic opulences,
for I never tire of hearing your sweet words.

THE *BHAGAVAD GITA* is the finest introduction to the spiritual tradition of India. It is unique among Eastern spiritual teachings because it celebrates the experience of God in the ordinary actions of everyday life. This mystical experience was traditionally thought to be open only to those who foresook the world for a life of prayer and meditation. The *Gita*, however, extends it to us all, encouraging us to remain in the world and to find God in our daily work. Such awareness calls us to live fully in the sanctity of every moment and brings with it the highest joy.

The *Gita* is arranged as a conversation between God and the soul, in the form of Krishna and Arjuna. This dialogue invites our reflection and exploration, and is always ready to tell us more, even after many readings. As Mahatma Gandhi wrote, "When doubts haunt me and I see not one ray of hope on the horizon, I turn to the *Gita* and find a verse to comfort me."

In the history of India the *Gita* occupies a unique place as the one universally accessible text acknowledged by all Hindus. How old is the *Gita*? In one sense it matters little, for its knowledge is born of eternity, and it is as alive today as it was when it was first spoken. Most modern scholars suppose it achieved its present Sanskrit form around 500 B.C.E. although according to Vedic tradition Krishna spoke the *Gita* 5000 years ago. The book records Krishna's message of love, woven into a powerful cosmology based upon the teachings of the world's earliest body of philosophical writings, the *Vedas* and *Upanishads*. The glorious vision of the *Gita* draws the sublime philosophy of the *Upanishads* into the practical path of yoga, uniting the outer world in which God reigns supreme with the inner world where God and the soul sit side by side, and brings us to the conclusion of surrender and devotion to God.

By the middle of the first millennium C.E., the *Gita* was adopted by Hindu teachers as their standard popular text, and by around 700 C.E. it had been singled out by the great Sankara for his famous commentary. All the principal Hindu teachers later commented on it, each according to their particular viewpoint. It was first translated into English by Charles Wilkins in 1785, and is said to have been published in over two hundred separate English editions. Henry David Thoreau wrote in 1854 of the "stupendous and cosmogonal philosophy of the *Bhagavad Gita*." Thomas Merton in the 1960s saw the *Gita* as "like the Gospels, teaching us to live in awareness of an inner truth. In obedience to that inner truth we are at last free."

THE SPIRIT OF HUMILITY The speaker of the *Bhagavad Gita* is Krishna, who reveals himself to be the Supreme Godhead. Krishna figures prominently in the vast *Mahabharata*, the epic history of ancient India, of which the *Gita* is but one episode. The *Gita* opens on the brink of a cataclysmic battle, the events of which are recounted in the *Mahabharata*. Krishna is asked by the warrior, Arjuna, to drive his chariot into the space between the two opposing armies. Here Arjuna despairs, and lays down his arms, turning to Krishna for spiritual help.

Arjuna's despair was due to the awful prospect of having to kill his own friends and family members, who stood in the opposing army. It is said that Arjuna was an enlightened soul placed in illusion by Krishna, and his experience thus parallels our own: God allows us to fall into the illusion of material life, so that we can learn better who we really are and who we really wish to be.

The physical site where the *Gita* was spoken is Kurukshetra, eighty miles north of Delhi, but the spiritual place where it can be heard, that inner space of emptiness and doubt, is one we all know.

ABOVE IN THE SPACE BETWEEN THE TWO ARMIES, ARJUNA TURNS TO KRISHNA FOR SPIRITUAL HELP.

ABOVE THE AMBER FORT REFLECTED IN THE LAKE AT JAIPUR—IN THE MIDST OF LIFE WE MUST REFLECT ON KRISHNA'S WORDS.

We all have our battles to fight, brought on by illusion. The most difficult battle is the one we wage daily with our own mind and senses. But even in the midst of adversity we must find the time to pause, as Arjuna did between the opposing armies, to contemplate the mysteries of life and what it is we really seek, opening ourselves to hear the voice of the spirit. In order to do this, to make this radical shift in awareness, we need help. When reading the *Gita*, we should remember that it is spoken in such a rare moment, to one who has put aside certainty and pride. The spirit of humility that allows us to ask for help is easier to speak of than to practice, yet to learn spiritual truths it is essential to open the heart.

DIALOGUE OF THE SPIRIT Having asked for help, Arjuna enters a dialogue of the spirit. He places his earnest questions, and Krishna patiently answers them. One way that this dialogue arises in the life of the spiritual seeker is through learning from a teacher. Since ancient times, aspirants began their search by finding a guru. Whether one is fortunate enough to find a guru or not, the dialogue of the spirit ultimately takes place on the inner plane. All of life is a conversation, in which God and the individual soul respond to each other. God responds to our desires, allowing us to discover more of himself and his energies, and we can open more of ourselves to him. The connection between the soul and God is a gift, and this is the heart of Krishna's teaching. Once this is understood, all actions become expressions of our inner connection with God.

THE STRUCTURE OF THE *GITA* The first six chapters begin with an analysis of the self, establishing each being as eternal, reincarnated from one body to another in the search for liberation from the cycle of birth and death. Then comes the art of yoga: how to live and act in a way that leads to liberation and to union with God. Krishna teaches three paths of yoga: *karma* yoga, the path of action, working without attachment to the results of one's work; *jnana* yoga, the path of knowledge of the spirit through study and contemplation; and *bhakti* yoga, the path of devotion to God. Krishna stresses that all three lead to the same goal, yet he concludes by recommending *bhakti* yoga.

The middle six chapters describe the transcendent Supreme Being. They contain the heart of the *Gita*; four seed verses in Chapter 10, verses 8–11, which describe Krishna as the source of all, and the divine life shared by his devotees that transforms every act into a sacred offering of devotion leading to the encounter with Krishna. Chapter 11 contains the famous vision of the Universal Form—one of the greatest mystical visions in world literature. This central section of the *Gita* again concludes with devotion to Krishna, described in poetic detail in Chapter 12.

The final six chapters further elaborate these themes, adding a detailed explanation of the three material qualities of goodness, passion, and darkness, showing how these qualities manifest in daily life, and including in Chapter 16 an intense and cautionary account of the effects of the quality of darkness. The last chapter concludes, from verse 55 onward, with a glorious affirmation of Krishna's love and his final assurance to the traveler on the path: "Abandon all kinds of religion and surrender to me alone. I will free you from all sinful reactions. Do not fear."

WHO IS THIS BOOK FOR? This new edition of the *Bhagavad Gita* is intended for anyone exploring the spiritual path, from whatever faith or persuasion. I have made a completely fresh translation from the Sanskrit, aiming at simplicity and clarity, and I have added the short commentary of a seeker of truth in the modern world. The *Gita* is extremely condensed: each Sanskrit verse is a pithy statement that builds upon the last, developing complex and interwoven ideas into a closely argued philosophical framework. It utilizes standard Vedic concepts such as karma and yoga that could be studied at length. I have not dispensed with the verse format, allowing each verse to stand alone as a focus for the reader to ponder on, though in translating into simple English I have simplified the nuances of the original Sanskrit text.

I learned the *Gita* from my teacher, Srila A.C. Bhaktivedanta Swami Prabhupada. His commentary and translation of the *Gita* is intended for dedicated students, and in it he sets absolute standards of knowledge and devotion. However, he encouraged his followers (in his commentary on 4.3) to write their own devotional commentaries on the *Gita*. I therefore began this *Gita* as a way of giving the great book to my own children, and in response to requests for a simple retelling of the *Gita* that would be universal in its appeal.

When I first encountered the *Gita* I was struck by Krishna's voice. Having been brought up to revere the voice of God in the Bible, I had not been told about Krishna's words in the *Gita*. Yet here the same voice of God was unmistakable; I indeed felt the book fulfilled its name: *Bhagavad Gita* means "Song of God." Many who read the *Gita* for the first time will regard Krishna as a mythological figure, whose words symbolize the voice of God or the inner wisdom of the soul. Other readers will feel faith in Krishna as the incarnation of God who lived in Northern India 5000 years ago, as a cowherd boy who later became a prince of the Yadu dynasty.

Whether you approach the *Gita* as a seeker after truth and wisdom, whose mind is open to hear a new voice, or as a faithful devotee of Krishna seeking his grace, this edition is intended for you, for in this dialogue of the spirit the choice always rests with each of us. As Krishna says to Arjuna:

> *Thus I have told you this most secret of all secret knowledge.*
> *Reflect over this fully, and then do as you wish.*

1

ARJUNA'S DILEMMA

The armies of the Kurus and the Pandavas prepare to face each other in a battle that will engulf them in destruction. The great warrior Arjuna, full of foreboding, asks Krishna to drive his chariot between the two armies, where he is assailed by doubt and confusion.

ON THE BRINK OF BATTLE

The *Bhagavad Gita* comes to us through the mouth of
Sanjaya, who is gifted with the psychic ability to see and
hear faraway events—in this case on a distant battlefield.
Thus it is clear this dialogue has a mystical origin.

King Dhritarashtra wants to know what will become of
his sons. They and their cousins, the sons of Pandu, both
lay claim to the throne, and after years of enmity the two
sets of brothers have at last come together to settle their
differences on the battlefield. They are joined on either side
by the military powers of the known world, many of whom
are related to one or both parties, and all of whom are
gathered in one place ready to fight to the point of death for
their chosen heroes. Such is the fate of the powerful: they
brush their rivals aside to gain power, then they in turn are
crushed to make room for others. Only Krishna is not part of
this remorseless struggle. He is neutral: he wants nothing
yet he loves all.

The scene opens with Dhritarashtra, the blind and aging
monarch, seated near the great field where his sons will do
battle with their cousins. He inquires of his trusted secretary:

1   *O Sanjaya, what happened once my sons and the
     sons of Pandu had assembled at the holy field of
     Kurukshetra ready to fight?*

Sanjaya replied:

2   *Once Prince Duryodhana had seen the Pandava
     armies arrayed against him, in battle formation,
     he spoke to his teacher.*

Duryodhana said:

3–11 *My teacher, look upon the armies of the Pandavas,
      commanded by your wise disciple, Dhristadyumna.
      Here are many heroic warriors equal to their leaders
      Arjuna and Bhima, such as Yuyudhana, Virata, Drupada,
      Drstaketu, Cekitana, Kasiraja, Purujit, Kuntibhoja,
      Saibya, Yudhamanyu, Uttamauja, the son of Subhadra,
      and the sons of Draupadi. All of them are powerful
      chariot fighters. But hear of our own generals, highly
      qualified to lead our army. There is yourself, Bhisma,
      Karna, Kripa, Asvatthama, Vikarna, and Bhurisrava,
      son of Somadatta. You are all sure to be victorious.
      Besides you there are many other heroes ready to die
      for my cause. They are all powerfully armed and highly
      experienced military men. Our strength under the
      protection of Grandfather Bhisma cannot be measured,
      whereas the Pandava's strength under Bhima is limited.
      All of you must now support Bhisma, standing at your
      appointed places ready for battle.*

ABOVE KRISHNA AND ARJUNA SOUNDED THEIR DIVINE CONCHES.

OPPOSITE A PILGRIM AT THE SOURCE OF THE GANGES. SPIRITUAL PRACTICES GIVE THE ABILITY TO SEE FAR-OFF EVENTS.

With these words Duryodhana fell silent.

12–19 *The mighty Bhisma, grandfather of all the fighters on both sides, sounded his battle conch like the roar of a lion and gladdened Duryodhana's heart. The Kuru army vibrated their conches, war drums, and horns, making a tumultuous sound. On the opposite side Krishna and Arjuna sat in a great chariot drawn by four white horses. They sounded their divine conches named Pancajanya and Devadatta, and Bhima blew his great conch Paundra. Prince Yudhisthira and his fighting companions— among them Nakula, Sahadeva, the King of Varanasi, Sikhandi, Dhristadyumna, Virata, Satyaki, Drupada, the sons of Draupadi and the son of Subhadra—all blew their conches. The combined vibration filled the earth and the sky, shattering the hearts of their opponents.*

A more dramatic setting for spiritual teaching could hardly be imagined. The battle will last eighteen days and develop into the most awesome contest of fighting men recorded in ancient history. Yet paradoxically they have chosen a sacred place, the field of Kurukshetra, for this conflagration.

Reconciling the apparent contradiction between the sacred and the profane is a fundamental concern of the *Bhagavad Gita*.

War arises in every generation, like a forest fire that cannot be stopped, causing ordinary people to kill their friends and brothers. It is no accident that such a desperate and confusing time should be chosen by Krishna for delivering his teaching on how to bring an end to suffering.

SURVEYING THE ARMIES

20 *Arjuna stood in his chariot, his bow held at the ready. After scanning the army of the sons of Dhritarashtra, he turned to Krishna.*

Arjuna said:

21–23 *Infallible One, take my chariot between the armies so that I can see who has come here to defend the evil-minded Duryodhana, and with whom I will have to fight.*

Sanjaya narrated:

24–25 *Obedient to Arjuna's request, Krishna brought the mighty chariot into the middle of the two armies, halting in front of Bhisma, Drona, and the chieftains of the world.*

Krishna said:

Just behold, Arjuna, all the Kurus assembled here.

26–27 *Before him on both sides Arjuna recognized fathers, grandfathers, uncles, brothers, sons, grandsons, teachers, and friends. When he saw all these familiar faces confronting one another, he was filled with deep compassion and sadness.*

Arjuna had not wanted this war. So it is with each of us: we may not seek conflict, but in response to the choices we make in our lives it often seeks us. Arjuna has made his choices, and Krishna has become Arjuna's chariot driver to lead him wherever he wishes to go. In the same way God does not interfere with our choices, but helps us fulfill them. He accompanies each of us as the impartial observer of all we do, presenting us with choices and respecting our freedom—and should our choices lead us into difficulty he is there, unseen, to protect us if we fall.

13

CHAPTER 1

30   *I can hardly stand up and my mind is reeling; I foresee only disaster.*

31   *No good can come from killing our families. I want no such victory, Krishna, nor the happiness or rewards it might bring.*

32–35 *What value has power, happiness, or life itself when the ones with whom I would share them—teachers, grandfathers, fathers, sons, grandsons, uncles, and brothers—are here to lose everything and die? They may wish to slay me, but I will not kill them even for the whole world.*

36   *Guilt will haunt us if we kill them. Though Dhritarashtra and his supporters are aggressors, they do not deserve death. What happiness could we find by killing our own brothers?*

37–38 *Blinded by greed, these men see no wrong in killing their family or friends, yet surely we have the wisdom to shun such a sinful act.*

39   *When families are broken, their traditions and duties disappear, and as a result immorality spreads.*

40   *With the spread of immorality, the chastity of women is lost, causing the social order to disintegrate.*

41   *Such disintegration makes hell for everyone—its victims and its perpetrators. Even the departed souls, deprived of the prayers and offerings of their families, fall from peace.*

42   *So the breakdown of the family makes the very foundations of community fall apart.*

43   *Moreover, Krishna, I have heard it said that those whose family traditions are destroyed are destined to live in hell.*

44   *How terrible that our greed for earthly power should drive us to such sinful deeds as the destruction of our own families.*

45   *It would be better if the sons of Dhritarashtra come with their weapons and kill me, unarmed and unresisting.*

THE PROSPECT OF DISASTER

Arjuna said:

28   *Dear Krishna, when I see these kinsmen in front of me ready to fight, my limbs weaken and my mouth is parched.*

29   *My body shivers, my hairs stand on end, my bow slips from my grasp, and my skin burns.*

Sanjaya concluded:

46 *Speaking so, in the midst of that battlefield, Arjuna dropped his weapons and sank into his chariot, overcome with grief.*

This opening chapter of the *Bhagavad Gita* is set in an ancient society, yet the issues of morality and social order that concerned Arjuna still concern us today. Justice and defense of the oppressed are obligations for us all, especially in times of conflict when ordinary safeguards break down. Some believe justice requires the application of violence, whereas others, seeing that one person's aggressor is another's father, brother, or son, believe forgiveness is the better way. These are the moral dilemmas that have beset humanity since the first human hearts beat together.

A central part of the functioning of Vedic society was the offering made to ancestors to ensure their progress in the

ABOVE THE CALM VOICE OF TRUTH ENTERS LIKE CLEAR SUNLIGHT ON A DARKENED ROAD.

OPPOSITE DEVOTEES AT A WAYSIDE SHRINE — OFFERING PRAYERS FOR THE DECEASED IS AN ESSENTIAL PART OF TRADITIONAL SOCIETY.

afterlife. Today the offering of prayers for deceased parents and friends is still a significant part of the culture of many societies all over the world.

Faced with the prospect of tragedy, Arjuna's heart says one thing and his head another. Confusion and emotion battle in his warrior's chest. This is the context for the *Bhagavad Gita*. The calm voice of truth must enter like clear sunlight on a darkened road. The stage is set for Krishna to teach Arjuna, and through him all troubled or inquisitive souls who would listen.

2

UNDERSTANDING THE SOUL

The warrior lays his weapons at Krishna's feet and begs for help. Krishna encourages him, for the soul as passenger in the body is eternal and can never be slain. He introduces yoga as the path to freedom and lasting peace.

ARJUNA'S SORROW

1   *Arjuna was overcome with compassion and sorrow,
    and his eyes filled with tears. Seeing this, Krishna
    began to speak.*

The Blessed Lord said:

2   *Dear Arjuna, how has this despondency come over
    you in the hour of crisis? This does not become a
    noble person like you. It will lead you not to heaven,
    but to disgrace.*

3   *Do not give in to this frailty. It does not become you.
    Abandon this weakness of heart and prepare to fight.*

The tears of Arjuna mark him as one who is ready to hear
spiritual truths. In times of crisis, when the uncertainties
and pain of this world bear down, we may at last be ready
to part the veil of material illusion and uncover the truth.
However, though tears are a sign of compassion, they are
also caused by illusion. We long to relieve the suffering
of the body and mind, but we do not know how. The body
and mind are only the outer dress of the eternal self. If we
wish to end suffering, we must care not just for the body
and mind, but also for the inner, eternal self. This eternal
self will be the main subject for Krishna's first discourse.

   We are reminded here that the speaker, Krishna, is
Bhagavan, which means "Possessor of Opulence." During his
life on earth he radiated the six opulences of beauty, wisdom,
strength, wealth, fame, and detachment. For those ready to
hear, his words will resound with these qualities to drive
away illusion and its companion, suffering.

SUBMISSION BEFORE KRISHNA

Arjuna replied:

4   *O Krishna, how can I aim my arrows at men like
    Bhisma and Drona, who are worthy of my worship?*

5   *I would rather become a beggar than kill these
    great souls who are my teachers. If for the sake of
    worldly gain I kill my superiors, my victory will be
    stained with their blood.*

LEFT THE BURNING GHATS AT VARANASI — ONE WHO KNOWS THAT THE SPIRIT IS
ETERNAL HAS NO NEED TO LAMENT FOR THE BODY.

6   *I do not know which is better: to conquer them or to be conquered by them. If I were to kill the sons of Dhritarashtra who stand before me, I would have no more reason to live.*

7   *I am confused about my duty and overwhelmed with fear and weakness. I surrender to you as your disciple and beg you to teach me what is best for me.*

8   *Nothing will drive away this burning sorrow, even if I win an unrivaled kingdom on earth with the powers of a god.*

9   *Krishna, I shall not fight.*

With these words the great warrior fell silent.

10   *Between the two armies Krishna smiled and spoke to the sorrowful Arjuna.*

The Blessed Lord said:

11   *You speak learned words, but you mourn for something not worth your sorrow. The wise do not lament for the living or the dead.*

Arjuna is now ready to accept Krishna as his spiritual teacher. When we are overwhelmed by life's complexities, we do well to accept help with openness and humility. To learn from a teacher one must abandon pride and, like Arjuna, we must ask for guidance. This is the right spirit with which to hear Krishna's words in the *Bhagavad Gita*.

Krishna smiles because he is confident he will soon dispel his friend's misery, but he does not comfort Arjuna. Instead, Krishna's words are uncompromising and direct, because his purpose is to teach the truth. The body must die, whereas the spirit inside the body is eternal. One who knows this has no need to lament for the body, which is a temporary covering for the self.

THE SELF IS DIFFERENT FROM THE BODY

12   *There never was a time when I, you, and all these warriors did not exist, and there never will be a time when any of us shall cease to be.*

13   *As the self moves in this body from childhood to youth to old age, so the self passes into another body at death. The wise are not confused by this change.*

Here is the essential understanding of reincarnation. Krishna describes all those present as separate eternal beings who pass from one temporary body to another. Each of us can experience this process of change for ourselves. We see our childhood body change to that of an adult, and our adult body to that of an old person. This ancient knowledge of physical change is demonstrated by modern science, according to which the cells in our bodies are replaced approximately every seven years. Despite these changes of body, we still feel ourselves inwardly to be the same person: the inner self does not change. When at last the outer body dies this inner self moves on to enter a new body.

19

TOLERATE THE IMPERMANENT

14   *Happiness and distress appear and disappear like winter and summer. They arise from the perceptions of the senses and you must learn to tolerate them without being disturbed.*

15   *When one is undisturbed by happiness and distress and is steady in both, one is fit for eternal life.*

16   *The unreal has no permanent existence, whereas the real exists forever without change. So conclude seers of the truth who have studied the nature of both.*

Although we are eternal beings we experience through our senses and mind the ever-changing conditions of this temporary world, from the cold of winter to the heat of summer. If we practice patience in the face of the pleasures and pains of life and the happiness and distress they bring, we will learn to distinguish the firm ground of truth, which is eternal, from the tides of illusion.

THE ETERNAL SOUL

17   *That which pervades the body is indestructible. No one can destroy the imperishable soul.*

18   *The body in which this eternal, indestructible, and immeasurable soul lives must come to an end. Therefore fight, Arjuna.*

19   *Some think the soul is slayer, some think the soul is slain. Both are wrong, for the soul is neither slayer nor slain.*

20   *The soul exists forever in the present, having no birth or death. The soul is the oldest, without beginning or end, and is not killed when the body is killed.*

21   *When one knows the soul to be indestructible, eternal, without birth or change, how can one possibly kill or induce anyone else to kill?*

ABOVE WE EXPERIENCE THE SUN BY ITS WARMTH AND LIGHT. IN THE SAME WAY THE LIFE IN THE BODY REVEALS THE SOUL WITHIN.

22   *As a person exchanges old clothes for new, so
      the soul abandons old bodies to enter new ones.*

23   *The soul cannot be cut by weapons, burned by
      fire, drenched by water, or withered by wind.*

24   *This soul cannot be pierced, burned, wet, or dried. For
      the soul is everlasting, all pervading, unchangeable,
      and immovable, staying eternally the same.*

25   *It is said that the soul is invisible, inconceivable, and
      unchangeable. Knowing this, you should not lament.*

By nature's law, whatever is born must die. But the soul
has no birth and hence no death: the soul is life. We can
perceive the presence of the sun, even when it is hidden
behind clouds, by its warmth and light. In the same way
we can perceive the presence of the soul by the life the
soul gives to the body. This life we call consciousness and
it is indestructible.

Here is further explanation of the process of reincarnation,
through which the soul takes on new identities, as an actor
changes dress to play new parts. This change of body is
made possible by the grace of God, who fulfills our desires
as one friend fulfills the desires of another. He accompanies
each one of us from one body to the next on our journey
through the universe. Though we are forgetful, he knows our
past, present, and future, and his words in the *Bhagavad
Gita* are to awaken us to who we really are.

The individual soul is a fragment of the Supreme Soul,
a spark of the divine fire. As a spark possesses the qualities
of the fire in minute proportion, so each soul possesses
in minute quantity all the qualities of the Supreme Soul.
As the Supreme Soul is indestructible, so is each and every
particle. Each soul has a unique identity, never to be lost
or dissolved. The awakening of the soul's eternal identity
as a companion of God is the greatest goal of life.

DO NOT LAMENT

26   *O mighty-armed Arjuna, even if you believe this soul
      is forever born and forever dying, still you should
      not lament.*

27   *One who is born must die, and one who dies must
      be reborn. Do not mourn the inevitable.*

28   *All beings are invisible in the beginning, visible in the
      middle, and invisible in the end. Why grieve over this?*

ABOVE WHEN THE BODY AGES, THE SOUL ABANDONS IT FOR A YOUNG BODY, AS WE
DISCARD OLD CLOTHES FOR NEW.

29   *Some have direct experience of the soul, whereas
      some hear or speak about the soul. All these find the
      soul wonderful. Others, though they hear about the
      soul, cannot understand at all.*

30   *The one who lives in the body can never be killed.
      Therefore you should not lament for any living being.*

The soul is a thing of wonder, yet most of us are too
preoccupied with the external world to contemplate it.
Without knowing who or what we are we struggle for
existence, unaware that the solution to all our problems
is to be found through self-understanding.

Krishna's words, spoken on a battlefield, leave no room
for sentimentality. Everything in this world must disappear
in the end. However, the deliberate taking of life, of whatever
species, interferes with the destiny of another creature and is
an act of aggression. Such an act will produce its own reaction
for the perpetrator, even though the soul lives on unharmed.

21

THE HONORABLE WARRIOR

31   *Do not hesitate in your sacred duty as a warrior. For
      a soldier nothing is more sacred than the fight for a
      just cause.*

32   *Fortunate is the warrior for whom this opportunity
      comes, opening the doors of heaven.*

33   *If you do not take up this just fight, you will fail in
      your duty and your honor will be lost.*

34   *People will forever speak of your shame, and for one
      who has been honored, dishonor is worse than death.*

35–36 *The great warriors who gave you honor will think you
      have fled the battlefield. They will scorn you and your
      enemies will deride you. What could be more painful?*

37   *If you die in battle you will enter heaven. If you
      win you will enjoy the earth. Therefore rise and
      fight with determination.*

38   *Fight for the sake of fighting. Look equally on
      happiness and distress, gain and loss, victory
      and defeat. In this way you will not incur sin.*

It is the duty of the strong to protect the weak, and the
scriptures promise birth in heavenly realms to a warrior who
dies fighting for such a just cause. These realms lie above
the earthly plane but still within the material world. There
are many levels of existence within the material world of
birth and death.

In this world of birth and death we are all warriors, called
to daily action in the struggle of life, where every action
produces a reaction that binds us to the cycle of rebirth.
Karma yoga is the art of work with no reaction. The literal
meaning of the Sanskrit word *karma* is "action" or "work,"
and it can also mean the reactions to work that bind the soul.

Krishna here completes his teaching about the soul.
He will now teach how the soul should act to get free
from the binding ropes of *karma*.

THE PATH OF FREEDOM

39   *Now I have taught you in detail about the soul. Next,
      hear about yoga, or work without attachment. When
      you act with this knowledge you can free yourself
      from the bondage of action.*

40   *On this path there can be no loss or disappointment,
      and even a little progress will free you from great fear.*

41   *Those on this path are resolute and single-minded.
      The thoughts of those who lack such determination
      branch endlessly in all directions.*

Human life offers freedom from the cycle of birth and death through spiritual development. Even a little progress along the path of spiritual development lasts forever, whereas material development brings only temporary benefits. At the very least, spiritual activities guarantee a human birth in the next life, from which further spiritual progress can be made. Thus we are saved from the fear of descending into non-human species in the next life.

When our activities are connected to Krishna through awareness of him as the goal, our lives achieve a unity of purpose that is deeply satisfying. Without such unity of purpose the mind will be full of endless desires, and we will never be at peace.

BEYOND THE REWARDS OF PARADISE

42–43   *Those without knowledge are drawn to the rituals and ornamental words of the scriptures and to the rewards they promise, such as birth in paradise. They long for pleasure and power and care for little else.*

44   *Carried away by their love of pleasure and power, they lack the inner resolve for spiritual life.*

45   *The rituals of religion belong to this world. Rise above them, Arjuna, above the dualities of pleasure and pain and ambition for profit and security. Be fixed in truth and centered in your inner self.*

46   *For one who knows the ocean of truth, these rituals are no more than a small pond in the midst of a vast flood.*

The scriptures of the world speak to us on many levels. The hymns of the *Vedas* promise rewards in the gardens of paradise, and the scriptures of other religions offer similar promises, but none of these rewards will last forever. If we are still attached to pleasure and power, we will have to remain in the world of birth and death, even after experiencing the pleasures of paradise.

For those willing to go beyond the world of dualities to discover their true selves, the *Vedas* include the *Upanishads* and the *Bhagavad Gita*. These sacred texts lead from the world of the temporary to the world of the eternal. The goal of all scriptures is to remember God. A life overflooded by remembrance of Krishna's name has no need for the rituals of religion or the rewards they bring; these rituals appear as a small pond in the presence of the ocean.

The results of actions are called by Krishna the fruits of work. Every action produces a result, just as a tree produces fruit. Some fruits are sweet, some bitter. Those who want to enjoy the fruits of their work must stay in this world to fulfill their desires. In this way selfish work binds us to the cycle of birth and death. Even good deeds, if performed with attachment, can draw us back to this world to taste their results, and so the soul continues in the cycle of birth and death. The tendency to selfish action can be overcome by working in *buddhi* yoga— constant awareness of Krishna.

As will be elucidated in later chapters, Krishna is the root of all existence. When the root of the cosmic tree is watered, the leaves and branches are nourished. By working for Krishna we benefit ourselves and the whole world. This is the key to happiness and the end to suffering. This kind of work, offered to Krishna in loving service, leads to direct communion with the Lord in the heart.

LEAVING THE FOREST OF DELUSION

51   *The wise, who serve the Lord with love, free themselves from the cycle of birth and death by letting go of the results of their actions. So they reach the place beyond all miseries.*

52   *When your intelligence has passed out of the dense forest of delusion you will become indifferent to all that has been heard and all that is to be heard.*

53   *Your mind will be secure in self-knowledge and undisturbed by the voices of doctrine and ritual. Then you will have achieved true yoga.*

The sense of personal ownership in this world is an illusion, for all belongs to God. Those who understand this leave aside attachment for earthly possessions and are released from the world of birth and death. Many have trod this path of detachment, inspired by love for God, and their example and words go before us.

THE ART OF ALL WORK

47   *You have the right to work, but not to its results. Do not be attached to the fruits of work, or to not working.*

48   *Work with a spirit of detachment, being equal to success or failure. Such evenness of mind is called yoga.*

49   *Through the practice of yoga, avoid selfish activities and surrender yourself to the inner guidance of the Lord. Those who seek rewards from work find no happiness.*

50   *One who is inwardly guided by the Lord passes beyond good and bad actions. Therefore strive for yoga, the art of all work.*

THE UNDISTURBED ONE

Arjuna asked:

54   *How will I recognize one who has understood the self? How would such an enlightened one sit, or move, or speak?*

Krishna said:

55   *One who does not dwell on the desires in the mind, but finds satisfaction within, is deep in knowledge.*

56   *One who is undisturbed by misery, not craving happiness, free from attachment, fear, and anger, is a sage of steady mind.*

57   *One who is without affection for good or evil, meeting both without praise or blame, is secure in wisdom.*

Inner concentration and stillness, called *samadhi*, is the first symptom of the enlightened soul. This state of mind overcomes the craving for material pleasure that is the cause of so much unhappiness. In the world of matter, in which the senses predominate, the mind gravitates toward sense enjoyment. However, if one finds spiritual happiness within, one finds a contentment more satisfying than anything sense enjoyment can offer. In this position the natural good qualities of the soul develop of their own accord. A person who lives in this way is freed from attachment, fear, and anger and accepts the good and bad of this world equally as the mercy of God.

THE POWER OF THE SENSES

58   *One who withdraws the senses from the world, as a tortoise draws in its limbs, is secure in wisdom.*

59   *One may renounce external pleasures but still desire to enjoy them. Such desires cease only when one tastes the higher reality.*

60   *The senses are so strong that they can carry away the mind even of a wise person striving to subdue them.*

RIGHT A WISE PERSON LIVES SIMPLY, WITHOUT AFFECTION FOR EITHER GOOD OR EVIL.

61   *One who restrains the senses and whose thoughts are focused on me is secure in wisdom.*

62   *While dwelling on the objects of the senses, one develops attachment for them. From attachment grows desire, and from desire arises anger.*

63   *Anger produces illusion, and from illusion comes forgetfulness. Forgetfulness brings loss of intelligence, and when intelligence is lost one falls down again into the whirlpool of material existence.*

The senses make good servants but bad masters. It is natural to want to enjoy through the senses, yet such enjoyment brings suffering in its wake. This is the puzzle of material existence. While setting forth on the spiritual path one must bring one's senses under control by following regulations, as a sick person must follow a restricted diet in order to get healthy. This means avoiding excessive gratification of the senses. But unless one tastes the inner satisfaction of the soul the taste for material pleasures will remain, and any amount of artificial restrictions will be useless, or even counterproductive.

FREEDOM IN SELF-CONTROL

64   *One who practices self-control, who engages with the world without attraction or aversion, achieves the mercy of God.*

65   *This mercy ends all miseries. In this serene state the intelligence soon becomes clear.*

66   *One without self-control cannot have a clear intelligence or a steady mind. An unsteady mind finds no peace, and without peace where is joy?*

67   *As a strong wind sweeps away a boat on the water, so the mind dwelling on even one of the senses carries away the intelligence.*

68   *Therefore one whose senses are under control is secure in wisdom.*

The self-control of yoga brings freedom from attraction and aversion, the opposing forces that govern material life. One must sacrifice the apparent freedom of sense gratification to gain the real freedom of inner peace that comes by the grace of God.

In the yoga of devotion, the senses are controlled not by force, but by attraction to the higher principle of loving service to Krishna. The eyes of devotion see that everyone in this world is dear to Krishna, and Krishna is the dearest friend of everyone. This simple truth provides a calm center for the mind, and so lasting peace and happiness.

RIGHT SHORE TEMPLE AT MAHABALIPURAM — THE OCEAN, THOUGH FILLED BY RIVERS, REMAINS STILL, LIKE THE MIND UNDISTURBED BY DESIRES.

BELOW ON THE RIVER AT VARANASI — THE BOAT OF THE MIND CAN EASILY BE CARRIED AWAY ON THE WATERS OF THE SENSES.

PEACE IN THE NIGHT

69　*The night of the world is the time of awakening for the self-controlled, and the time of awakening for the world is night for those with inner vision.*

70　*One who is undisturbed by the flow of desires finds peace, as the ocean—though filled by incessant rivers—remains still. One who strives to satisfy those desires finds no peace.*

71　*One who gives up selfish desires, who lives content, without ego or possessiveness, achieves peace.*

72　*This is the spiritual path, on which one will not be deluded. If one follows this path, even at the hour of death, one will enter the presence of God.*

Lasting peace is found in the presence of God. God is present everywhere, and we are always in his presence, but we are generally not conscious of this. The flow of desires and our attachment to them obscure our perception of God's presence. The essence of Krishna's advice in this second chapter is to let go of selfish desires. Then it will be possible to perceive the presence of God, and the will of God.

Those who are unaware of God's will live in illusion, and their day seems like night to the God-aware. Conversely, to materialists, those who try to serve the will of God seem to have missed the whole point of life: their day also seems like night. Thus a tension always exists between the spiritual and the material ways of life, and Krishna's teaching is a challenge to the material way.

Service to God is satisfying to the soul, so satisfying that it fills the spiritual aspirant with an inner peace, deep and still like the ocean. In this state the flow of material desires, so avidly promoted by the commercial interests of today's world, passes unnoticed.

Desires cannot be negated: they are natural to the soul. The soul yearns for the presence of God because each soul is a child of God and shares in his spiritual nature. We do not have to wait for death to enter the presence of God. We have only to absorb ourselves in his loving service to have already attained the spiritual kingdom. This can take many lifetimes or it can be achieved within a second.

3

KARMA YOGA
–WORK AND DESIRE

Offerings made to the Lord or to the heavenly beings bring us fulfillment in the cosmic cycle of sacrifice. The real enemy to be slain is not the opponent on the field of battle, but selfish desire, enemy of the wise and destroyer of self-understanding.

THE NEED TO ACT

Arjuna said:

1   *Krishna, if you think knowledge is superior to action, why urge me to fight this terrible battle?*

2   *I am confused by your contradictory words. Please tell me clearly which path will lead me to the highest good.*

The Supreme Person said:

3   *Arjuna, long ago I explained two paths of faith in this world: the contemplative are inclined to the path of knowledge, and the active to the path of service.*

4   *One cannot gain freedom by avoiding work, or perfection simply by renouncing.*

5   *No one can be still for even a moment, for all are compelled, even against their will, to act according to their natures.*

6   *One who outwardly controls the senses but inwardly dwells on sense enjoyment is deluded and is a pretender.*

7   *But one who inwardly controls the senses while outwardly working without attachment is on the right path.*

8   *Perform your duties, for action is better than inaction. Without work one cannot even maintain the body.*

Activity is fundamental to the self, for the nature of the soul is to give to others and ultimately to give to the Lord. Therefore we must all work if we are to be happy. Work that seeks to control others or take from them creates conflict and unhappiness, whereas work in the spirit of service leads the soul toward satisfaction and knowledge.

Knowledge and action belong side by side in spiritual life, for philosophy without faith is dry speculation, and faith without philosophy is sentiment, which can give rise to fanaticism. Philosophy and honest work are both necessary.

THE WHEEL OF SACRIFICE

9   *Do your work as a sacrifice for Vishnu; otherwise it will bind you to this world. Work for his sake and you will always be free.*

10   *In the beginning the Creator sent generations of beings into the world along with sacrifice, saying, "Be happy and prosper, for sacrifice will bring you all that you desire."*

11   *The heavenly beings, nourished by your sacrifice, will also nourish you. Pleasing one another, you will all achieve the highest benefit.*

12   *Satisfied by your offerings, those heavenly beings will give you all you wish for. But one who enjoys their gifts without giving in return is a thief.*

13   *Gentle people who offer their food before eating are released from all sins, but the unfortunate who cook only for themselves eat suffering.*

14   *Life is sustained by food grains. Food grains are nourished by rains. Rains depend on sacrifice, and sacrifice is born of work.*

15   *Work comes from the* Vedas, *and the* Vedas *arise from the Supreme Godhead. Therefore the all-pervading Transcendence is eternally situated in acts of sacrifice.*

16   *So turns the wheel of sacrifice. One who lives selfishly, who delights only in the senses and does not care for the turning of this wheel, lives in vain.*

Gifts such as rain and food are not be taken for granted. They depend on the great cycle outlined here by Krishna. All work, even the daily toil for survival, forms part of this cycle, called here the wheel of sacrifice. We work so as to take our part in the cosmic cycle, which in turn guarantees us all we need. Our survival depends not on the results of our own work, but on the goodwill of the heavenly beings, called Devas. Their service to God is to look after our needs, and we in turn offer them service. Life is thus a constant process of giving and receiving in which we all depend upon

ABOVE THE GREAT CYCLE OF LIFE GIVES US THE RAINS THAT HELP TO BRING FORTH OUR FOOD.

each other for happiness and security. Those who neglect this cosmic cycle, in Krishna's words, "live in vain."

To understand how to harmonize our work with this cycle we need the guidance of Krishna, or his devotee. The universe teaches how to live in this spirit, and its books of guidance are the *Vedas*, breath of the Lord. The original *Vedas* are in the form of Sanskrit hymns, but their wisdom is enshrined in scriptures and inspired books all over the world. They point the way to happiness in this world and lead us to spiritual enlightenment. By living in this world in accordance with divine wisdom we can fulfill our desires while deepening our relationship with the Supreme Lord, so that at the end we will enter the kingdom of God.

The underlying principle of offering to the Devas is accomplished by offering our actions to the Supreme Lord, who is the root of all existence. For example, prayer, or the simple chanting of God's names, transforms all work into divine service. Another simple sacrifice is the daily offering of our food to God. Food that is eaten in this consciousness will loosen the bonds of *karma* and purify our existence. Prayer and eating sanctified food is enough to transform our whole existence.

31

WORK WITH DETACHMENT

17   *However, one who finds pleasure within, who is illuminated within, who is satisfied in the self alone —such a person has no need to work.*

18   *This person has nothing to gain or lose by working or by not working, and does not depend on any being for anything.*

19   *Thus do your work without attachment, for by working without personal motive you will reach the Supreme.*

The sign of the enlightened state of consciousness is that a person finds pleasure within. The nature of the soul is to seek pleasure. Thus, so long as we do not taste that inner peace, called here *atmarati*, "pleasure in the self," we will be, drawn to the external pleasures of the world and will bind ourselves to the cycle of attachment. By tasting inner happiness we are freed, and our path becomes clear to work for the sake of the Lord, unattached to personal gain. In this stage our work is revealed to us from within, self-illuminated by the grace of the Lord.

THE WELFARE OF ALL

20   *Janaka and others reached perfection by working in this way. In the same way, for the welfare of all, you should act.*

21   *Whatever a great person does, others imitate. The standards set by the great are followed by all the world.*

22   *I have no duty, nor is there anything in all the three worlds that I need or want—yet even I work.*

23   *For if I did not work tirelessly, surely all humans would follow my path.*

24   *If I were not to work, the worlds would fall into ruin, and I would cause chaos that would destroy the peace of all beings.*

25   *As the ignorant act for themselves, so the wise should also act, but selflessly, for the benefit of the world.*

The work of maintenance is hidden from the maintained, as parents' efforts in running a household are hidden from their children. Thus we cannot understand how Krishna works for our welfare. Yet if we observe the wonders of his creation we can see everywhere signs of his care for all beings. God's work sets the pattern for us all. By working in a spirit of selflessness, for the benefit of others, we can share in the nature of God and be freed from the ties of this world.

LEFT WASHING CLOTHES BY THE RIVER—THE DAILY WORK OF MAINTENANCE GOES ON UNNOTICED, AS DOES THE CEASELESS WORK OF THE LORD.

DO NOT UNSETTLE THE IGNORANT

26   *A wise person does not disturb the minds of the*
      ignorant who are attached to their work, but rather
      acts in the spirit of devotion, encouraging them to
      do the same.

27   *Material nature does everything. Yet the soul deluded*
      by ego thinks "I am the doer."

28   *One who knows the truth, Arjuna, sees how nature*
      acts, and becomes detached from the senses and
      their objects.

29   *Bewildered by nature's ways, fools are caught up in*
      her works. Yet the wise should not unsettle those
      whose understanding is incomplete.

ABOVE THE WISE CAN HELP TO TEACH OTHERS BY SETTING AN EXAMPLE
FOR THEM TO FOLLOW.

So long as we remain in the illusion of material life, we
attach ourselves to the material body and take it for granted
that we are doing everything by ourselves. We are unaware
that all our actions are made possible by the Lord, and that
we can do nothing on our own.

Generally souls in this world are absorbed in their
activities like dreamers in their dreams. Each soul has a
particular course to pursue, and only when the time is right,
when the illusion becomes too painful or too plain, will the
soul be ready to perceive another reality. Then, as a sleeper
awakens when called by name, the soul can awaken on
hearing the name of Krishna.

33

CHAPTER 3

CHOOSE FREEDOM

30   *Devote your actions to me and fix your mind on the Self.
     Forgetting selfish desires, fight without hesitation.*

31   *Those who follow this teaching of mine, faithfully
     and with open hearts, are freed from the bondage
     of karma.*

32   *But be assured that those who have no regard for
     these teachings and do not follow them will be
     misguided and lost.*

We cannot be happy without God. The Supreme Lord is the
Soul of all souls and our existence depends on him. Yet our
spiritual nature is to be free. The resolution of this paradox
is to choose freely the service of God. This means to choose
the way of loving and giving, for only that will make us
happy. This is what Krishna wishes us to understand when
he says, "Devote your actions to me, fixing your mind on the
Self," for he is the Self of our self.

Faith in the Lord's orders, even if we are not perfect in
following them, is enough to bring liberation—this is
Krishna's promise. It is a matter of intention and disposition,
not performance. Sincerity of purpose is all that is asked,
for we each have our own nature and limitations, as Krishna
will explain.

If we choose to disregard the Lord's teachings, as they
are found in the *Bhagavad Gita* or other sacred books of the
world, God will not interfere with our choice. By so deciding,
we choose to remain under the spell of the illusions of the
material world until we are ready to choose again.

WALK THE PATH GIVEN TO YOU

33   *Even the wise act according to their natures,
     for all beings follow nature. What can repression
     accomplish?*

34   *Attraction and repulsion, that govern the senses, are
     obstacles on your path—do not let them rule you.*

35   *The occupation given to you, though imperfect,
     is better than another's, even perfectly done.
     Defeat one's own path is better, for another's path is
     dangerous.*

It is best to have the humility and honesty to acknowledge
our conditioning and work honestly from our natural level,
rather than try to be other than we really are. For example,
one whose nature is practical should not artificially try to
be intellectual.

Accepting the path meant for someone else, whether it is
more, or less, demanding than our own, and denying our
own nature and disposition, is misleading and will lead to
disappointment and frustration.

The process of spiritual development is a gradual
one, not abrupt. If we patiently follow the recommended
process a time will come when we may transcend material
considerations and be able to attempt anything for the sake
of Krishna.

THE ENEMY WITHIN

Arjuna said:

36   *Krishna, what drives people to commit sinful acts,
     even unwillingly, as if by force?*

The Lord said:

37   *It is desire, born of passion and later transformed
     into wrath, that is the all-devouring sinful enemy
     of this world.*

38   *As fire is covered by smoke, as a mirror by dust, as
     an embryo by the womb, so knowledge is covered
     by desire.*

39   *Thus knowledge is veiled by desire, the eternal
     enemy of the wise, which is never satisfied and
     burns like fire.*

40   *It lives in the senses, the mind, and the intelligence,
     using them to cover knowledge and bewilder the
     living being.*

41   *Therefore first control your senses, Arjuna,
     then slay this sinful destroyer of knowledge
     and self-realization.*

42   *The senses are elevated, but above them is the mind,
     and above the mind is the intelligence; yet the self is
     even higher than the intelligence.*

43   *Knowing yourself to be transcendental to the
     intelligence, steady the lower self by the higher
     self and defeat this formidable enemy called desire.*

Desire, in the form described here as the enemy, is called *kama* in Sanskrit. However the spiritual form of desire is called *prema*, "divine love," which is the original basis of all emotions. When the soul's eternal love is directed toward the Lord's creation instead of to the Lord himself it is transmuted into kama, or material desire. This *kama*, when frustrated, produces anger.

So long as we are under the control of material desire we will have to gratify the demands of the mind and senses, and we may feel some happiness in return. But this happiness is limited and temporary, and is the enemy of the true self because it leads to frustration.

Thus in the material world the living entity is bound by the golden shackles of *kama*, particularly in the form of sexual desire. No amount of gratification will satisfy *kama*, just as no amount of fuel added to a fire will extinguish it.

When the soul's search for pleasure in matter is at last baffled, the soul will be ready to discover the real nature of the self. This inquiry is the start of the spiritual path, and is the most important quest of human life.

The process of restoring true knowledge begins with understanding the difference between the self and the body, and with meditation upon the Supreme Lord. When the intelligence and mind are thus steadied and restored, we can gradually bring the senses under control. Thus *kama* can be transmuted back into love and the enemy slain.

BELOW DESIRES ARISE FROM PASSION, LIKE SMOKE RISING FROM EARLY MORNING FIRES, AND CLOUD OUR CLEAR VISION OF THE SOUL.

4

TRANSCENDENTAL WISDOM

Krishna reveals himself as the Lord of all beings, descended to earth to reestablish the teachings of yoga. He teaches us how to act without acting, thus burning *karma* to ashes. The ship of this knowledge will carry us over the ocean of misery.

ABOVE THE SUN IS HONORED BY ALL FOLLOWERS OF VEDIC CULTURE.

DESCENT OF WISDOM

The Blessed Lord said:

1   *I taught this eternal yoga to Vivasvan the sun god; Vivasvan gave it to Manu, father of mankind; Manu passed it to King Iksvaku.*

2   *Thus handed from one to another, it was known by saintly kings. But over a great passage of time this yoga was lost to the world.*

3   *Now I am teaching the transcendental secret of this ancient yoga to you, Arjuna, because you are my devotee and my friend.*

The Vedic civilization, like other ancient civilizations, saw its past as a time of wisdom lost to a later age. In modern times we should be wary of regarding old knowledge as inferior to our own. Truths do not change, only our perception of them. A new truth to one person may be an old truth to another.

The Vedic rulers claimed descent from the Sun and hence they took the name *Suryavamsa*, meaning "dynasty of the Sun." They brought the knowledge of yoga to earth, by their calculations two million years ago in the reign of Iksvaku, and it was revived by Krishna when he taught Arjuna five thousand years ago. To safeguard and teach this wisdom, which gave meaning and order to human life, was the sacred duty of the Suryavamsa.

Krishna chose to teach yoga to Arjuna because Arjuna was devoted to him. Devotion, or love and respect, is the quality that makes a person receptive to spiritual wisdom. Scrutiny and inquiry are necessary in the search for truth, but they come best from a mind and heart open to hearing answers. The way to understand Krishna is the same as the way to understand any person—with love.

KRISHNA'S MISSION

Arjuna said:

4   *Vivasvan was born long before you. How am I to understand that originally you taught him?*

The Blessed Lord said:

5   *Arjuna, both you and I have both passed many births. I remember them all, but you do not.*

6   *I am the Lord of all beings, without birth or death, yet still I appear in this world in my original divine form.*

7   *Whenever and wherever there is a decline in religion and a rise of materialism—at that time I descend myself.*

8   *To protect the good, to subdue those who do harm, and to reestablish the principles of religion, I appear in every age.*

9   *One who understands the nature of my divine birth and actions is not reborn after leaving this body, but comes to me, Arjuna.*

As the sun appears to rise and set, so the Lord appears to be born and to die. And like the sun, the Lord is seen in many lands and many epochs, for he expands in countless forms while remaining One. When he descends into this world, he speaks the truth in a way that can be heard by the people of that place and time. He appears personally or he sends his son or his servant. Krishna, Gautama Buddha, and Jesus are among his divine appearances.

Krishna appears in this world in his eternal spiritual form, which is one and the same with his Self. We each share in Krishna's nature, yet we forget ourselves when we enter the cycle of birth and death. Krishna never forgets: he remembers everything, always and everywhere. In his many descents into this world, Krishna brings his eternal companions, such as Arjuna, who was with Krishna when he spoke to the sun god, millions of years previously. As Krishna accompanies Arjuna through many births, so he accompanies each of us as our silent helper and protector. Without him this world would fall into ruin, and without his silent love and support we would be lost.

FREEDOM FROM FEAR AND ANGER

10   *Freed from attachment, fear, and anger, with mind absorbed in me and illuminated by me, many sought refuge in me, and so gained love for me.*

11   *As they seek my shelter, so I reveal to them my love. All beings, everywhere, are on my path.*

12   *Those in search of worldly success serve the gods of this world. For here on earth the results of work come quickly.*

13   *According to their natures and work, I divided humans into four classes. Yet though I did this, know that I am changeless and do nothing.*

14   *Work does not affect me; nor do I seek its rewards. One who knows this truth about me is not bound by work.*

15   *Long ago, those seeking freedom worked with this understanding. So should you, following their ancient example.*

Krishna created the path, or the many paths, upon which we all walk. Whatever a person's desires, Krishna allows and facilitates those desires. He is the friend of all.

People desire wealth or fame, and for it they sacrifice to the gods and the powerful of this world, but the rewards they receive are limited and temporary, and attachment to them brings fear and anger. Frustration, repression, fear of failure, fear of realizing oneself—these symptoms arise when we attach ourselves to the temporary forms of the material world and forget our eternal identities.

Therefore Krishna advises us to continue working, but without attachment and with knowledge. For the paths and ways of work created by him are formed so as to encourage us to rediscover our real natures, and again share with love and freedom in Krishna's spiritual existence.

The path to spiritual enlightenment will demand all our determination. Yet Krishna assures us that many have trod this path in the past and been successful. The encouragement of fellow spiritual travelers is essential, and even in this modern age, many have walked and are walking this difficult path.

BELOW THESE MYTHICAL ANIMALS DRAW THE CHARIOT-TEMPLE AT KONARAK, DEDICATED TO THE SUN GOD VIVASVAN.

22   *One who is satisfied with gain that comes of its own accord, who is above the dualities of this world, free of envy and steady in success and failure, though working, is not bound by* karma.

23   *For one who relinquishes all attachment, absorbed in knowledge, acting only in sacrifice, all work merges into transcendence.*

24   *A person absorbed in spiritual work sees the whole process of sacrifice—the giver and the gift, the offering and its acceptance—as pure spirit, and so enters the spiritual nature.*

HOW *KARMA* WORKS

16   *What is action and what is inaction?—this question confuses even the wise. I shall teach you about action, so you can be free from harm.*

17   *The ways of action are hard to know. You must learn to distinguish action, forbidden action, and inaction.*

18   *One who sees inaction in action, and action in inaction, is truly wise and on the spiritual path, though doing all kinds of work.*

19   *One whose enterprises are without selfish motive, whose karmic reactions are consumed in the fire of knowledge, the wise call learned.*

20   *One who renounces the results of work, being content and self-sufficient, though fully occupied in work, does nothing at all.*

21   *One who is without motive, with mind and intelligence controlled, with no sense of ownership, though working to sustain life, incurs no sin.*

The true nature of work is divine. To put this understanding into practice, three kinds of work must be distinguished: work to be avoided, work that binds, and work that frees.

Work to be avoided comes under four moral restrictions in Vedic culture: meat-eating, gambling, intoxication, and promiscuous sex. In these liberal times, these restrictions may seem too demanding, but the principle behind them is clear enough: any activity that needlessly harms or exploits another living being, or your own self, should be avoided.

Work that binds and work that frees are made clear by Krishna: work done with attachment to the results will bind, and work done without attachment to the results will bring freedom.

We can visualize the entire cycle of work—the worker, the endeavor, the instruments, the intention, and the result —as *Brahman*, the divine energy of God. Originally all is *Brahman*, or spirit, and only when it is used selfishly does it appear to be material. Recognizing the spiritual origin of everything transforms our lives, and the same work that once caused bondage becomes the cause of liberation.

Work in this spirit is possible when we have faith in the protection of God. When we act in accord with the divine cycle of sacrifice described by Krishna in the third chapter, the Lord looks after all our needs. Knowing this, we can place our welfare in his hands, accept whatever gain comes of its own accord, and work for the welfare of all beings. Thus we are free.

WAYS OF SACRIFICE

25   *Some mystics give sacrifices to the heavenly beings, and others give them in the fire of the Supreme Spirit.*

26   *Some give the senses, such as hearing, in the fire of self-restraint, and others give the objects of the senses, such as sound, in the fire of the senses.*

27   *Some give the work of the senses, and of the life force, in the yogic fire of the controlled mind, to gain knowledge of the self.*

28   *Others give their possessions, or perform penances, or practice yoga, or study the Vedas while following strict vows.*

29   *Others, inclined to breath control, give their outward breath to their inward and their inward breath to their outward, stilling both. Or they fast and offer the outward breath to itself.*

30   *All these who understand sacrifice are released from their sins. They enjoy the results as divine nectar, and enter the eternal spiritual nature.*

31   *Arjuna, without sacrifice you cannot live happily in this world or the next.*

32   *These ways of sacrifice are laid out by the Vedas. They all arise from action: know this and you will be free.*

33   *Better than sacrifice of material possessions is sacrifice in knowledge, for work culminates in knowledge.*

These verses use the imagery of the Vedic fire ceremony, in which oblations such as ghee and grains are offered into the flames. The fire represents the Supreme Being, and the oblations represent the fruits of work. This ritual is performed by Hindu priests, but Krishna extends its symbolism to all walks of life, saying that any work done in the spirit of sacrifice is as good as the sacred fire ceremony. Thus, with mindful action, the whole world and all work within it become sacred.

Krishna describes types of sacrifice: to the Devas who supply means of life, such as water, heat, and light; to the impersonal *Brahman*, sacrificing one's own identity; hearing and chanting sacred mantras; restraining sensual life; practicing the *astanga* yoga system (the eightfold path of mysticism taught by Patanjali, which includes meditation with focused vision and controlled breathing) to raise the consciousness, or *hatha* yoga to discipline the mind and body; fasting; pilgrimage; and studying scripture. Through such activities, human life offers a route out of the material world for those who wish to take it. Though there are many kinds of happiness in this world, all of which bind the soul to the cycle of birth and death, surpassing them all is the happiness of the liberated spirit.

THE GIFT OF KNOWLEDGE

34   *Learn from the wise with submission, inquiry, and service. The self-realized souls who have seen the truth will give you knowledge.*

35   *Once you have received the truth, you will never again fall into illusion, and you will see all living beings in me, the Self of all.*

36   *Even if you are the worst of all sinners, the boat of knowledge will carry you over the ocean of miseries.*

37   *As a blazing fire turns wood to ashes, so the fire of knowledge burns to ashes all karmic reactions.*

38   *In this world, nothing is so pure as knowledge. In time, the mature mystic discovers this knowledge from within.*

39 *A faithful person, dedicated, with senses
    subdued, soon achieves knowledge and attains
    transcendental peace.*

40 *An ignorant, faithless, and doubting person is lost.
    The doubting soul cannot find happiness in this world
    or the next.*

41 *One who through yoga renounces action, whose
    doubts are dispelled by knowledge, who lives in
    the self, is not bound by work.*

42 *Therefore, Arjuna, with the weapon of knowledge
    remove the doubts in your heart. Armed with yoga,
    stand and fight.*

Knowledge is the key, and the way to acquire it is to listen
with earnest humility to those who have seen the truth.
This is Krishna's advice. Faith in a superior source of
understanding is essential to finding happiness. We
cannot doubt everything and be happy. We must try to
put our trust in the scriptures and in those who live their
messages. Personal association with such souls will bring
this knowledge to life. As Krishna said at the beginning of
this chapter, the knowledge of yoga was treasured and
passed from one king to another in exactly this way, and
continues to be passed on by the Lord's devotees living in
this world.

If you are unable to meet an enlightened soul, then place
your trust in Krishna. By reading his words in the *Bhagavad
Gita* you are hearing directly from your inner guide, who is
with you all the time. Krishna is the air we breathe, the
space through which we converse, the sense of touch by
which we reach out to one another. He is the Self within
all, and by knowing him we are in touch with all beings
everywhere. To know Krishna is the aim of life, and he is
the boat to carry us over the ocean of miseries.

5

LIFE OF FREEDOM

As a lotus leaf sits on the surface of a pond without becoming wet, so the soul illuminated by wisdom lives in this world in freedom and joy. This wise soul sees all beings as equal and knows the Lord as the friend of all.

ABOVE BY HONORING GOD WE WATER THE ROOTS OF THE TREE THAT SUSTAINS US.

FREEDOM THROUGH WORK

Arjuna said:

1   *Krishna, first you recommend renouncing work,
    then working in yoga. Tell me clearly which is best.*

The Blessed Lord said:

2   *Renouncing work and working in yoga both lead to
    liberation. But of the two, working in yoga is better.*

3   *The true renouncer feels neither hatred nor desire,
    and freed of these dualities easily escapes bondage.*

4   *The ignorant speak of yoga as different from the
    contemplative path. Yet a true follower of one
    of these paths achieves the results of both.*

5   *The position reached by the contemplative can
    also be reached by the one who works in yoga. One
    who sees contemplation and action as the same,
    sees truly.*

6   *Without the practice of yoga, renunciation is difficult.
    But a thoughtful person devoted to the practice of
    yoga soon achieves the Supreme.*

7   *A pure soul devoted to the practice of yoga, who
    controls the mind and senses, whose self is united
    with all selves in the Supreme Self, though always
    working, is not entangled.*

Krishna has explained that work in knowledge is called inaction, or *akarma*, because it is without karmic reaction. Now Arjuna asks for further clarification.

To practice yoga, in any form, is to seek closer union with God. The essential point here is that the attempt to renounce the world, or to be detached from the results of actions, will succeed if we positively attach ourselves to God by acting in the awareness of God's presence. Yoga is more than theory: it is practical action.

Krishna is the soul of the world, and contemplation means to find him as the root of the tree. Having found the root, yoga is to water the root by acting in awareness of God. One who sees all beings as part of God feels love for all and is loved by all. By watering the root, the leaves are nourished, and thus service to Krishna is service to all.

ENLIGHTENMENT

8–9   *A person in divine consciousness sees, hears,
      touches, smells, eats, moves, sleeps, and breathes,
      while all the time thinking, "I do nothing." For
      speaking, evacuating, receiving, and opening or
      closing the eyes are only the interactions of the
      senses with their objects.*

10   *As the lotus leaf is untouched by water, so one who
      works without attachment, devoting all actions to
      the Lord, is untouched by sin.*

11   *Abandoning attachment, followers of yoga use
      their body, mind, intelligence, and senses for
      self-purification.*

12   *One in divine consciousness lets go of the results
      of work and finds unbroken peace. The faithless one
      attached to the fruits of work is bound by desire.*

13   *The soul who mentally gives up all actions, doing or
      causing nothing, lives peacefully as ruler of the city
      of nine gates.*

14   *This ruler of the body does not create actions, or
      cause their fruits, or induce others to act. All is done
      by nature.*

15   *The all-pervading Supreme Spirit is not responsible
      for the sinful or pious actions of the living beings.
      They are bewildered because their understanding
      is covered by ignorance.*

16   *As the sun lights up everything in the
      daytime, knowledge dispels ignorance and
      reveals everything.*

17   *When intelligence, mind, and faith take refuge in the
      Supreme, knowledge cleanses away all misgivings,
      and one passes beyond the land of rebirth.*

Knowledge removes the illusion of material life to reveal
the self as pure soul, different from the body, and united
with all life in the Supreme Lord. Such awareness illuminates
everything and brings peace, for even though we may be
active in so many ways, if our actions are dedicated to the
Lord they bring freedom.

The body is a gift of the Lord. As long as we identify
ourselves with this city of nine gates (eyes, nostrils, ears,
mouth, anus, and genitals) we are bound by it, but as soon
as we identify with the Lord, who also dwells within the
body, and use the body in his service, we are free.

The Lord is the constant companion in our heart, and
he perceives our desires without interfering with them, as
a person smells the perfume of a flower without physical
contact. He is impartial, and even though we are in illusion
he does not limit our independence. He helps us fulfill our
desires in such a way as ultimately to bring us nearer to him.

BELOW LIKE THE SUNRISE, DIVINE KNOWLEDGE ILLUMINATES ALL OF LIFE.

CHAPTER 5

SEEING WITH EQUAL VISION

18 *The wise see with equal vision a learned and gentle priest, a cow, an elephant, a dog, and an outcaste.*

19 *Those whose minds are balanced and even have already overcome rebirth. They are flawless like* Brahman, *and therefore exist in* Brahman.

20 *A person who neither welcomes the pleasant nor rejects the unpleasant, who is self-intelligent, unbewildered, and knows the science of God, is situated in transcendence.*

21 *A person unattracted to external pleasures, who finds happiness within, is absorbed in the Supreme and enjoys unlimited bliss.*

22 *Pleasures arising from the senses are the sources of misery. They have a beginning and an end, Arjuna, and the wise do not delight in them.*

23 *One who can withstand the urges of desire and anger while living in this body is well situated and happy in this world.*

If we learn to see all beings as divine, as part of the Supreme and therefore intimately connected with one another and with ourselves, we do not discriminate on the basis of species or form, or on the basis of caste, color, or creed. The Lord himself is the friend of every creature, dwelling inside their hearts and treating them equally without discrimination. If we can understand this, we also will feel friendship toward every being. Creatures who are less intelligent or weaker than us are even more deserving of our friendship. An enlightened person avoids giving pain to any animal, even to the smallest insect.

Entanglement in sensory pleasures is described here as contacting the sources of misery. Sense enjoyment in a regular and moderate way is a necessary part of life. But it is wise to control the body's demands for sense enjoyment because sense pleasures are addictive, and can be the cause of much misery.

The first step to spiritual consciousness is to recognize oneself as spirit, different from the body. Once we transcend the illusion of being the physical body, we can cultivate a steady mind unaffected by hatred and attraction. If we are not to lament at loss we must also not rejoice at gain. In other words, we must be steady in both by learning detachment from the body.

Of all pleasures in this world sex is the most sought after, and is the motivation, conscious or otherwise, behind most of what goes on in the name of society. A sign of spiritual advancement is to be neutral toward sexual attraction: one who is free from attachment to sex is free from attachment to material existence.

We are set apart from animals by our ability to enjoy spiritual realization, which is superior to material pleasure. The aim of human life is the pursuit of self-understanding, leading to the discovery of the natural bliss of the soul.

LIBERATION

24 *One whose happiness and joy are within, who is illumined within, is liberated in the Supreme and attains* Brahman.

25 *Sages devoted to the welfare of all living beings, freed from sins, finished with doubts, and with minds subdued, enter* Brahman.

26 *Ascetics freed from anger and desire, who are self-realized and self-disciplined, soon enter* Brahman.

27–28 *Excluding outward sensations, gazing between the eyebrows, suspending within the nostrils the inward and outward breaths, controlling the senses, mind, and intelligence—the contemplative intent on liberation becomes free from desire, fear, and anger, and is forever liberated.*

29 *One who knows me as the enjoyer of all sacrifices and austerities, as the Supreme Lord of all creation, and as the friend of all beings, attains peace.*

The blessed state of *brahma nirvana* is described here three times as the goal of sages and ascetics. It means to enter *Brahman*, or to merge oneself into the Supreme Spirit. Some wish for their self, like a drop of water, to dissolve into the ocean of the Supreme and cease to exist as an individual. They are advised to practice *astanga* yoga, the eightfold path of mysticism taught by Patanjali, which includes meditation with focused vision and controlled breathing.

Devotees of Krishna do not aspire for this passive state of spiritual existence. They long to realize their eternal individuality as souls united with God through love, and to realize their oneness with *Brahman* by entering into an eternal spiritual relationship with the Lord. The first step

48

toward this oneness is the devotee's practice of Krishna consciousness—remembering the Lord. When this remembrance becomes constant, all miseries are brought to an end because the soul becomes immersed fully in the Supreme.

The real cause of suffering in this world is forgetfulness of the Supreme Friend, and so those who are devoted to the welfare of all living beings try to revive Krishna consciousness in human society.

In concluding this chapter, Krishna summarizes knowledge—to recognize his presence as the enjoyer, the controller, and the friend, and as the goal of all our sacrifices in *karma* yoga. Since we all exist within the Supreme Lord we cannot enjoy this world without him. All peace will be ours when we know the One who is our supreme and innermost friend.

6

MYSTIC YOGA

The mystic, whose mind is still and peaceful,
is like a lamp in a windless place, and sees
God in all things. Such a perfect yogi, devoted
to Krishna, is never separated from him.

GIVING UP SELFISH MOTIVATION

The Blessed Lord said:

1   *One who works as required, without attachment to results, is truly renounced and is a yogi—not one who gives up work and worship.*

2   *Renunciation is the same as yoga, for yoga requires one to give up selfish motivation.*

3   *For a beginner in yoga, the path is work; for one advanced in yoga, the path is stillness.*

4   *One who abandons selfish motivation in sense enjoyment and action is elevated in yoga.*

Krishna encourages those who carry on with their lives, doing as they are called on to do, not drawing attention to themselves for the sake of recognition or profit, but working without attachment for the sake of goodness alone. These are the silent yogis who live in the midst of every community, whose internal relationship with God is more intimate than that of those who make a show of prayer, or meditation, or of abandoning the world.

Success in yoga depends on inner motivation and state of mind. While being outwardly busy and active, one may be inwardly still. In the popular practice of yoga, people start with physical exercises, which are meant to lead them on to the practice of inner stillness. In the beginning of the process work alone is the means. Then gradually, while working, inner stillness establishes itself within the mind. There Krishna is to be found.

This state of inner stillness or desirelessness can be achieved by understanding ourselves as part of the complete whole of all existence. No one is independent from the web of life, materially or spiritually, and our own interests can be served by working for the sake of the whole. One who sees the presence of Krishna in all of life sees all activities connected to the Supreme. The interest of the whole is served by working for the satisfaction of Krishna. This brings satisfaction to all of the parts. When we experience fulfillment by this method, we no longer find it necessary to pursue selfish desires or ambitions. We have achieved yoga: union with God.

MAKE THE MIND YOUR FRIEND

5   *Let your mind elevate you, not degrade you—for your mind can be your friend as well as your enemy.*

6   *If one subdues the mind, it is your friend; but if one fails to do so, it behaves as an enemy.*

7   *One with subdued and tranquil mind lives in the company of the Supreme Self, whether in happiness or distress, heat or cold, honor or dishonor.*

8   *One satisfied through knowledge and realization, whose senses are subdued, is established in yoga, and sees earth, stone, and gold as the same.*

9   *An elevated person looks on friends, enemies, relatives, colleagues, strangers, saints, and sinners— all as equals.*

The foundation of yoga is control of the mind. We must first learn to distinguish between ourselves and our mind. The mind is an instrument that can be used for both good or ill. A mind accustomed to obeying the demands of the senses leads into entanglement with material life. The natural function of the mind is to accept or reject, and it must be trained to accept beneficial things and reject harmful things. By training, our minds will gain a taste for pure foods, improving books, inspiring entertainments, enlightened company, and ultimately for service and devotion to God.

If the mind is clear of distractions it will naturally be governed by Krishna, and be the true friend and bringer of freedom. This is because it will not obscure the messages of the Supreme Self received within the heart. A clear mind, undistracted by the demands of the senses, is like a well-tuned radio receiver: it receives and communicates, free of background interference, the messages of God. One whose mind is tuned to this divine signal is always guided by the Lord.

When we recognize Krishna as the essence of all, we see the value in all, both moving and still, because all is part of Krishna. We do not condemn others for their actions, knowing that Krishna permits all to act as they desire without condemnation.

RIGHT WITH ENLIGHTENED VISION WE CAN SEE ALL THE WORLD, WHETHER STONES OR GOLD, ENEMIES OR FRIENDS, WITH PEACEFULNESS AND EQUANIMITY.

THE HAPPINESS OF THE YOGI

ABOVE A YOGI IS HAPPY TO BE ALONE AND WITHOUT POSSESSIONS,
FREE TO CONCENTRATE ON THE SUPREME.

10   The yogi, living alone in a secluded place with
     carefully controlled mind, free from desires and
     feelings of possessiveness, concentrates the whole
     self on the Supreme.

11–12   Practice yoga seated firmly on kusa grass covered by
        deerskin and cloth, in a sanctified place not too high
        or too low. Control the senses and fix the mind on one
        point to purify the heart.

13–14   Hold the body, neck, and head erect, gaze steadily at
        the tip of the nose, and with tranquil and subdued mind
        remain celibate and without fear. Thus meditate on
        me and sit absorbed in me as the highest goal of life.

15   Constantly absorbing the whole self in this way, the
     yogi of controlled mind reaches the supreme peace
     called nirvana, and lives with me.

16   *Yoga is not for one who eats too much or too little, who sleeps too much or does not sleep enough.*

17   *One who is moderate in eating, sleeping, working, and recreation banishes all sorrow through yoga.*

18   *One whose thoughts are restrained and rest in the self, free of all cravings, is established in yoga.*

19   *As a lamp in a windless place does not waver, so the yogi whose mind is controlled is steady in meditation on the self.*

20   *One whose mind is stilled by the practice of yoga sees the self through the pure mind and rejoices in the self.*

21   *One who reaches this state experiences boundless happiness through transcendental senses, and never leaves the truth.*

22   *Having gained this place one imagines no greater gain, and is unmoved even by great misfortune.*

23   *This perfect state untouched by suffering is called yoga.*

24   *Practice this yoga with unwavering faith. Completely forsake all other aspirations and control the senses from all sides with the mind.*

25   *Step by step, using firm intelligence, withdraw into trance. Fix the mind on the self alone and think of nothing else.*

26   *Wherever the mind wanders because of its flickering and unsteady nature, bring it back under the control of the self.*

27   *Thus with mind at peace, with passions calmed and freed from the burden of past deeds, the yogi gains supreme happiness and realizes* Brahman.

28   *Freed from all blemishes, the yogi who constantly practices yoga in this way easily achieves unlimited bliss in touch with the Supreme.*

Although not everyone can practice this system of mystic yoga, the basic principles set out here, such as fixing the mind on Krishna, controlling the senses, and following the path of moderation are relevant to all yoga practice.

To eat with moderation we can follow the yoga diet of vegetables, fruits, grains, and dairy products. These foods, combined in countless palatable recipes, simple or elaborate, are sanctified by being offered in devotion to Krishna. Such sanctified food is itself enough to bring a person to the goal of yoga. For all who aspire to union with God there is a path that will suit.

Nirvana means the end of illusion and the death of the illusory self. However, this is not the end of everything. For as the false self dies, the eternal soul experiences the boundless joy of the soul's own spiritual nature. This joy culminates in the experience of union with God, in which the soul chooses to live eternally in love with Krishna. This is the final goal of all yoga practice, whether it be the eightfold system of *astanga* yoga taught by Patanjali and described in this sixth chapter, or the devotional path of *bhakti* yoga taught by Krishna throughout the *Bhagavad Gita*.

SEEING GOD IN ALL BEINGS

29   *One absorbed in yoga, observing all beings equally, sees the Self in all beings and every being in the Self.*

30   *One who sees me everywhere and sees everything in me, never loses me and is never lost to me.*

31   *The mystic who sees me as one in all beings worships me with love and lives with me always.*

32   *One who sees oneself and all beings as equal, both in happiness and distress, is a perfect mystic.*

God is present everywhere throughout the spiritual and material worlds. The difference between spirit and matter is a difference of vision only: one who can feel God's presence everywhere sees everything as spirit.

Every being is a particle of the Supreme Spirit, and the Supreme Spirit accompanies and guides every being. So although externally, because of forgetfulness, we experience the illusion of separation from the Lord, he is never separated from us, nor are we separated from him. A mystic therefore offers love and respect to all beings, regardless of their outer appearance or their status, knowing that the Lord dwells within each of them as he does within one's own self, and that he favors all beings equally as a mother does her children. With this vision we understand that all beings, knowingly or unknowingly, serve God at all times.

THE RESTLESS MIND

Arjuna said:

33   *This yoga of equanimity you have taught seems unendurable for the restless mind.*

34   *For the mind is turbulent, strong, and obstinate, Krishna, and to subdue it is as difficult as to control the wind.*

The Blessed Lord said:

35   *Truly the wayward mind is hard to subdue, but with practice and dispassion it can be trained.*

36   *For one with uncontrolled mind, yoga is hard to attain. Yet I say that, with practice, one can succeed who strives with disciplined mind.*

BELOW THE TURBULENT MIND IS AS DIFFICULT TO CONTROL AS THE WIND.

The solitary practice of yoga as Krishna has described above is, in this day and age, possible for only a few rare souls. There is no record even of Arjuna having attempted it. If it was difficult in his day, it is surely even more difficult today, when modern conditions create so many intrusions to distract the mind and senses, and when we lack spiritual training from an early age or widespread support in the community for this kind of spiritual quest.

Yet still Krishna recommends that with practice the mind can be controlled. The best way to begin controlling the mind is by hearing from a teacher who knows Krishna. By hearing about Krishna one will gain attraction for him and lose attachment to material things.

With the help of such a teacher, one can bring the mind under the control of the intelligence. It is said in the *Upanishads* that the self is a passenger in the chariot of the body, which is pulled by five horses that are the five senses. Intelligence is the driver, and the mind is the reins controlling the horses. One whose intelligence keeps a firm hold over the mind, and so controls the senses, will be at peace and make progress in yoga.

The easiest way to control the mind in this age is to fix it on the sound of the Hare Krishna mantra, the great mantra for deliverance. This will place our minds with humility at the lotus feet of Krishna. If this is accompanied by eating food offered to Krishna, the mind will be pacified.

THERE IS NO SPIRITUAL FAILURE

Arjuna said:

37 *What is the fate of a person who begins on the path of yoga with faith but who loses determination and falls away, failing to achieve success?*

38 *Is not such a person, bewildered on the path to transcendence, lost to either world like a fragment of cloud that evaporates in the vastness of the sky?*

39 *This is my doubt, Krishna, and you are the only one who can remove it. Please dispel this doubt completely.*

The Blessed Lord said:

40 *A person of faith is not lost in this world or the next. One who does good, my friend, is never overcome by evil.*

41 *One who falls from the path of yoga enjoys countless years in the heavens of the pious, and is then born on earth in a good and fortunate family.*

42 *Or one is born in a family of transcendentalists full of wisdom. Such a birth is hard to find in this world.*

43 *There one's former divine consciousness is re-awakened, and one strives further toward perfection.*

44 *This spiritual seeker, carried effortlessly onward by the influence of former practice, passes beyond the conventions of religion.*

45 *Thus with sincere effort the yogi is purified and perfected through many births, and at last achieves the supreme destination.*

46 *A yogi surpasses those who practice penance, or learning, or ritual. Therefore, Arjuna, be a yogi.*

ABOVE AS CLOUDS EVAPORATE IN THE SKY, SO THE UNSUCCESSFUL YOGI APPEARS TO BE LOST—BUT IS NOT.

47 *Of all yogis, one whose innermost thoughts dwell in me, who faithfully serves me with devotion, is considered by me to be the greatest yogi.*

One may forgo the illusion of material security in order to serve the Lord, and then fall away from one's spiritual path, being apparently lost both to the spiritual and material worlds. But whereas material progress is lost with the end of this life, spiritual progress is never lost, even after many lifetimes. The path of spiritual growth continues from one lifetime to another, and therefore spiritual endeavors, no matter how incomplete, are never in vain. As soon as a soul expresses the desire to know Krishna, the universe responds to the soul's awakening search for the Supreme. From one lifetime to another the soul continues on the path back to Godhead, helped by the Lord and by the guides he sends.

Such souls, being already on the spiritual path, are naturally attracted to chanting the names of the Lord. They may appear uninterested in the outward formalities and rituals of religion, but once attracted to the lotus feet of the Lord, they do not forget his beauty and his mercy, and he does not forget them.

In the first six chapters of the *Bhagavad Gita* Krishna surveys the yoga path. This begins with *karma* yoga and progresses to include *jnana* yoga—the yoga of knowledge—and *dhyana* yoga—the yoga of meditation. Now, at the end of the opening section, Krishna concludes that *bhakti* yoga, devotional service to the Supreme Lord, is the culmination of all forms of yoga. In later chapters he will describe in detail the principles and practice of *bhakti* yoga.

7

GOD AND
HIS ENERGIES

Krishna teaches deeper knowledge. He is the
taste of water, the fragrance of the earth, and
the light of the sun and moon. A rare soul,
who after many lifetimes understands that
Krishna is all, surrenders to him and is
released forever from birth and death.

RARE KNOWLEDGE

The Blessed Lord said:

1   *Hear now, Arjuna, how by practicing yoga with your mind attached to me, making me your shelter, you can know me fully beyond all doubt.*

2   *I will teach you such knowledge and deep wisdom beyond which there is nothing more for you to know.*

3   *Among thousands of people, one may strive for perfection, and of those who achieve perfection, hardly one knows me in truth.*

Until now Krishna has taught about the self and the techniques to realize the self through different forms of yoga, ending the sixth chapter by saying that to concentrate the mind on him, and take shelter in him, is the best of all. Those spiritual seekers not ready to take this step of faith can follow the various paths of yoga outlined so far. For those who are prepared to place their trust fully in Krishna, he now speaks about himself and his energies.

The information given from here on is not available elsewhere. We may speculate about the nature and existence of God, but until we hear in faith directly from God himself we will remain in doubt. Most people are absorbed in experiencing material life and do not find time for understanding God, but even among those who seek to know him, God is hard to know unless we have faith to hear his words.

GOD'S ENERGIES

4   *My material energies are divided into eight: earth, water, fire, air, ether, mind, intelligence, and ego.*

5   *Besides this external nature is my internal nature, made up of the living beings who sustain the world.*

6   *All beings are born from these two natures. I am the origin of the entire universe and its dissolution too.*

7   *There is no truth superior to me. All rests on me, as pearls strung on a thread.*

8   *I am the taste of water, the light of the sun and moon. I am the syllable Om in the* Vedas, *the sound in ether, and ability in human beings.*

9   *I am the original fragrance of the earth, the radiance in fire. I am the life of all that lives, the penance of all ascetics.*

10 *I am the seed of all beings, the intelligence of the intelligent, and the power of the powerful.*

11 *I am the strength of the strong, free of passion and desire, and I am desire that accords with the spirit.*

12 *The states of goodness, passion, and darkness come from me, and are within me, though I am not in them.*

Reality is made up of God's energies. The material world is formed of his external energy, which is temporary, illusory, and sorrowful by nature. We conscious beings, who share the same nature as God, belong to his internal energy, whose natural qualities are *sat-cit-ananda*—"eternity," "knowledge," and "bliss." The differences between ourselves and Krishna are that he is unlimited and independent, whereas we are small and depend on him for our existence, as sparks depend on a fire. God and the living entity are one and different.

If we wish to see evidence of God we have only to look around us and appreciate the wonders of this world. It is easy to take these wonders for granted: we can easily overlook the taste of water, for its taste is present in everything, as the sweet smell of earth is the basis of all perfumed flowers and aromatic forests. So it is with the presence of God. He permeates everything and becomes invisible. All life is in him, yet it cannot contain him, because he is independent of all.

THE SEEKERS OF TRUTH

13 *Deluded by these three modes of being, the world does not know me, who exists forever above them without change.*

14 *This divine illusion, created by me of the three modes, is hard to overcome. But those who seek my shelter can pass beyond it.*

15 *Those who do harm do not seek my shelter: they are the foolish, the degraded, the bewildered, and the ones who have chosen the demoniac nature.*

16 *Among those who do good, four kinds serve me with devotion: they are the distressed, the seekers of wealth, the seekers of knowledge, and the wise.*

17 *Of these, the wise, ever united with me in pure devotional service, are the best. I love them dearly, as they love me.*

18 *They are all noble souls, but the wise I consider as my own self, for they are absorbed in service to me as the ultimate goal.*

19 *After many lifetimes, one in knowledge surrenders to me saying, "Krishna is all." Such a great soul is very rare.*

The material world exists under the spell of Krishna's illusory energy, which is known as *maya*. Souls who choose to experience life without God take shelter in the illusion of forgetfulness, and in this way God becomes hidden from them. Bound by the ropes of illusion in the shape of goodness, passion, and darkness, they enter various forms of life, and pursue their desires along never-ending paths. After a very long time spent searching for happiness in this way, a soul comes to understand that Krishna is all, and that there can never be any separation from him. Such a wise person surrenders to Krishna.

BELOW THE BLESSED LORD SAID: "I AM THE TASTE OF WATER AND THE LIGHT OF THE SUN AND MOON."

CHAPTER 7

MANY FAITHS

20 *Carried away by desires of all kinds, people give themselves to different gods and religious practices, according to their natures.*

21 *Whomever or whatever they wish to devote themselves to, I encourage their chosen faith and make it firm.*

22 *With this faith they worship and receive their desires, which in truth are granted by me.*

23 *Such rewards are temporary for those of small understanding. The worshipers of the gods go to the gods, and my devotees come to me.*

Krishna lives in the heart of every being in this world. He gives us freedom to desire as we please and he helps us fulfill our desires. We are responsible for our choices and must accept our own consequences in the form of *karma*. We should be careful what we choose. But whatever it is, Krishna encourages us along our chosen path, ensuring we receive whatever it is we truly seek, for he knows our desires better than we do, and responds to the deepest wishes of our souls. All paths eventually lead to him.

The gods referred to here are the Devas, or heavenly beings who govern the forces of nature such as the planets and natural elements. Many powerful entities exist within the universe far beyond our limited understanding or control, and if we devote ourselves to the service of such beings we may be rewarded by them, and even drawn to live in the realms they occupy in the higher material spheres. Besides these are whatever gods we imagine for ourselves, based on our aspirations for security and happiness. All of these, whether real or imaginary, are extensions of Krishna, for it is he who gives them their powers to reward our worship, or fulfill our dreams.

OPPOSITE KRISHNA ENCOURAGES US IN THE FAITH WE CHOOSE, AND GRANTS THE REWARDS WE PRAY FOR THROUGH OUR CHOSEN DEITY—IN THIS CASE, GANESHA, REMOVER OF OBSTACLES.

GOD IS HIDDEN

24 *Those who do not know me think that I am formless though now dressed in form. They are unaware of my supreme nature, which is changeless and supreme.*

25 *I am not revealed to all, being hidden by my spiritual potency. This bewildered world does not know me, the unborn and imperishable.*

26 *I know the past, present, and future of all beings, but no one knows me.*

27 *All beings who enter this world are born into delusion, bewildered by the dualities of desire and hatred.*

28 *Those who have acted well and put an end to harmful deeds are freed from these twin illusions and serve me with determination.*

29 *Those who take shelter in me, striving for release from old age and death, understand all about* Brahman, *the self and action.*

30 *Those who absorb their minds in me as the Supreme Lord, supporter of this world and its gods, and rewarder of all sacrifices, can know me even at the hour of death.*

The souls in this world are said here to be deluded by desire and hatred. These opposite emotions are akin to love and fear. Driven by these we inhabit our imagined world of opposites, desiring success and fearing failure, craving love and fearing rejection. As long as we are caught in this web God's existence remains a mystery to us. Though he knows us intimately within our hearts, better than we know ourselves, still we cannot see him because we have chosen not to. Yet as we become aware of our emptiness without him and learn to pray and offer service to the Lord, our fear falls away and we realize that in success or failure, in love or rejection, he is always with us.

At the moment of greatest fear, when all that we know is taken from us at death, the supreme good fortune a person can have is to remember Krishna and accept his shelter.

8

ATTAINING THE SUPREME

The future journey of the soul after leaving the present body is decided by the state of mind at the time of death. What we contemplate thus becomes our future. Those who pass away remembering Krishna live eternally with him in the world that is never destroyed.

CHAPTER 8

THE INGREDIENTS OF LIFE

Arjuna asked:

1   *O Supreme Person, what is* Brahman*? What is the self
     and what is action? What is this material world and
     what are its gods?*

2   *How does the rewarder of sacrifices live in the body?
     And how can the self-controlled know you at the time
     of death?*

The Blessed Lord said:

3   *The imperishable soul, called* Brahman, *is the self.
     The evolution of living bodies is called action.*

4   *The ever-changing physical nature is called the
     material world. The gods and planets that make up
     this world are the visible form of the Cosmic Person,
     and I, the rewarder of sacrifices, live in the heart of
     every being.*

At the end of the previous chapter Krishna spoke of himself as
the supporter of the material world and its gods, and as the
rewarder of sacrifices. He has also said that those who take
shelter in him understand all about *Brahman*, the self, and
action, and that they can know him at the hour of death.
Arjuna asks for more detailed knowledge about all this.

ABOVE THE COSMIC FORM OF GOD IS VISIBLE ALL AROUND US IN THE
MAJESTY OF NATURE.

Krishna will speak more about these things and teach
about what happens at the time of death and about the art
of dying. He will explain how he, as the rewarder of sacrifices,
lives in everyone's hearts and fulfills their desires.

The Cosmic Person is imagined in the Vedic hymns in
the form of the planets of the upper, middle, and lower
material realms, and their controlling deities. This universal
form of the Supreme Lord is meditated on by those who
experience God in nature, in the sun and moon, in the
oceans and other elements.

HOW TO DIE

5   *At the end of life, whoever departs the body
     remembering me attains my nature without fail.*

6   *Whatever nature one remembers while leaving
     the body, that nature one will attain.*

7   *Therefore, remembering me always, fight on.
     With your mind and intelligence fixed on me,
     you will surely come to me.*

8   *One who meditates with constant practice and
     unwavering mind on me as the Supreme Divine
     Person is sure to reach me.*

9 *Think of me as knower of all, ancient, the ruler, smaller than the smallest, support of everything, of inconceivable form, radiant like the sun, and beyond darkness.*

10 *When death comes, with unwavering mind absorbed in devotion and strengthened by practice of yoga, those who fix the vital force firmly between their eyebrows reach the Supreme Divine Person.*

11 *Ascetics who are free of passion practice celibacy so as to enter what the knowers of the* Vedas *call the Imperishable. I shall now briefly explain this path.*

12 *Closing all the doors of the senses, focusing the mind on the heart and moving the vital force to the top of the head, you are established in yoga.*

13 *Vibrating the sacred syllable Om, which is* Brahman, *and remembering me as you depart this body, you will reach the supreme destination.*

14 *For those who remember me without deviation, Arjuna, constantly serving with me with devotion, I am easy to obtain.*

Death is the final examination which requires a lifetime of preparation. Whatever the mind remembers at death will create the pattern of our next life. We cannot all at once remember God if we have spent a lifetime forgetting him. The way in which our lifetime has been spent, and the attachments we have formed in life, will naturally occupy our mind at the approach of death. If we practice remembering God in the course of our lives, our minds will naturally turn to him when death approaches.

This does not mean that we should give up ordinary occupations. Krishna does not advise Arjuna to stop fighting, but rather to think of him while fighting. This is the basic principle of devotional service: to perform our duties in life while thinking of Krishna.

Death is a continuous process: at every moment the mind is called upon to die a little, and the body nears its demise. It is best to be prepared at any time to leave this world: saints advise that we live each day as if it were our last, keeping in mind the important things. It is easy to be complacent and forget the precariousness of life, as we are reminded when a friend or loved one is taken away without warning. Awareness of mortality is not to be morbid, but to remember and honor the immortal self as the intimate companion of God.

ABOVE SAINTS ADVISE US TO BE READY AT ANY MOMENT TO LEAVE THIS WORLD.

The constant remembrance of Krishna is called Krishna consciousness, and has the power to sanctify any place. It is not necessary for the devotee to stay in a special sacred place because by service to Krishna anywhere can be made sacred. A devotee is able to serve and remember Krishna in all circumstances.

THE WORLD OF SAMSARA

15   *Those elevated souls who come to me find the
      ultimate perfection. They never return to this fleeting
      place of sorrows.*

16   *The material worlds, even Brahma's heaven, are
      places of endless rebirth, but reaching me one is
      never reborn.*

17   *Brahma's day lasts a thousand ages and his night is
      of the same duration. Know this and you know the
      meaning of day and night.*

18   *In Brahma's dawn all creatures awaken from their
      sleep, and when night falls they once more merge
      into slumber.*

19   *Again and again the day comes, and this host of
      beings is active, and again the night falls and they are
      helplessly dissolved.*

Day and night, like birth and death, or youth and old age,
are the dualities of this world that remind us we do not
permanently belong here. No one wants to die because the
nature of the soul is to live forever. Nor do we like change:
we are creatures of security and familiarity. Yet this world
forces change on us, and takes from us its comforts and
assurances, driving us in our search for lasting peace to
seek religion. It is not a sign of weakness or inadequacy
to want faith in something lasting. It is an admission of the
truth, that the ephemeral cannot satisfy the eternal soul.
The best course is to live for God, and to love him in all we
do and all we know. For he will never leave our side, and his
love will never be lost, even with the loss of this body.

    Those who live good lives are reborn on earth or elevated to
higher material realms in their next life. The highest such realm
is *Brahmaloka*, "the place of Brahma," chief of all the gods of
this universe. In the heavenly realms the souls remain for a
very long time: as long as their merit lasts. But eventually they
fall back down to earth, where the cycle of *samsara*, repeated
birth and death, continues. The only way to end this cycle is to
be liberated through the practice of yoga.

THE ETERNAL WORLD

20   *Above this dormant matter, hidden from view, is
      another, eternal nature. When all in this world
      is annihilated, that part remains as it is.*

21   *That hidden place is called the Imperishable and
      the Supreme Destination. Those who go there never
      return. That is my supreme abode.*

22   *The Supreme Person, in whom all beings rest,
      and who pervades the world, can be reached by
      unwavering devotion.*

The scriptures of the world tell us about the abode of God as
a place without death or anxiety where love reigns supreme.
This cannot be only the fanciful imagination of generations
of humanity, for unless such a reality exists we would feel no
need to imagine it. The idea of immortality could not evolve
in a world where all things pass, unless an intuition told us it
is so. If our nature is to die and be extinguished forever, why
should we yearn for eternal life? The most obvious cause for
this instinct is that life is real and death is but an illusion.

LEFT THE CYCLE OF REPEATED BIRTH AND DEATH IS SYMBOLIZED BY THE TURNING OF
THE STONE WHEELS OF THE SUN GOD'S CHARIOT AT KONARAK.

REACHING THE SUPREME

23   *Arjuna, I will now teach you the times during which, passing from this world, the mystic gains either rebirth or no return.*

24   *Knowers of* Brahman *who pass away during the influence of the fire god, in daylight, in the bright phase of the moon, in the six months when the sun travels in the north, go to* Brahman.

25   *Mystics who depart during the influence of the smoke god, at night, in the dark phase of the moon, in the six months when the sun travels in the south, after reaching the moon planet, are reborn on earth.*

26   *These paths of light and dark are taught in the* Vedas. *One is the path of rebirth; the other is the path of no return.*

27   *Yogis know these two paths, Arjuna, and are never deluded. Therefore be always fixed in yoga.*

28   *One who understands all this surpasses the merits earned by study of the* Vedas, *or by sacrifice, penance, and charity. This yogi reaches the supreme original abode.*

The *Bhagavad Gita* contains in synopsis all aspects of Vedic wisdom, including this passage about the bright and dark paths. The technique of passing from this world described here is meant for those with the power to choose their moment of death. For one devoted to God, however, every moment—bright or dark—is auspicious, since all is placed in God's hands. All we need to know on the subject of dying has already been spoken by Krishna in the words, "Remember me and you will come to my abode."

As an aid to remembering Krishna one can practice chanting the *mahamantra*: *Hare Krishna Hare Krishna Krishna Krishna Hare Hare, Hare Rama Hare Rama Rama Rama Hare Hare.* This prayer occupies the mind, the tongue, and the sense of hearing, and is the ever-present direct and simple means of connecting with God. Its regular practice is pure yoga, taking the place of all other spiritual disciplines, which are very difficult in this age, and preparing us for life and for death.

RIGHT THE CONTINUAL CHANGING OF DAY INTO NIGHT IS A REMINDER OF THE IMPERMANENCE OF OUR EXISTENCE.

9

MOST CONFIDENTIAL KNOWLEDGE

The greatest secret of all is that Krishna, who is everywhere and in whom all beings exist, calls for our love and offers us his support and protection. Whatever we offer to him with love he will accept, thus releasing us from the bonds of *karma*, to live with him.

HEAR MY SECRET

The Blessed Lord said:

1   *Arjuna, I will teach you the greatest secret because you are willing to hear me with trust. Once you grasp this knowledge and its application, you will be released from all miseries.*

2   *This secret is the summit of education, the innermost secret, the supreme purifier, and the perfection of religion. It can be learned by direct experience, and be easily and joyfully practiced forever more.*

3   *Those with no faith on this path do not attain me. They return to the world of birth and death.*

ABOVE LEARNING TO TRUST OTHERS AND HEAR THEIR SECRETS PREPARES US TO HEAR THE SECRET VOICE OF GOD.

The more we are open to hearing from Krishna, or from his devotee, the more he can teach us. What Krishna has to teach is the secret of life. If we know this secret, even the hardest experience can seem easy and joyful, but without it the easiest thing becomes hard. Those who know the secret of Krishna consciousness may appear to live, work, and play like others, but by living for Krishna they are gaining freedom, whereas those living only for themselves are prolonging their attachment to matter.

The secret is told to Arjuna because he is trusting and has opened his heart to Krishna. We must choose how we want to be. Life gives reasons not to trust others, and also reasons to show trust. Sometimes others fail us; at other times they give to us. It is our choice whether to see our cup as half empty or half full.

The greatest question of trust is whether or not we are prepared to trust in a caring God. If things seem to go wrong in life, some choose to think that there is no God or that God is unfair. But sometimes what appears to be misfortune turns out to be good fortune in the long run. It may take a very long time to be in a position to know truthfully the full consequences of an act or an experience. One who chooses to trust God, even in difficult times, believing he is still there, giving protection and love, has chosen trust and is a devotee of God. When we are baffled by life, and unable to understand or control what is happening, we may be willing to let go and place ourselves with an open heart in the hands of God. Then, as we open to God and to life, the secret of life opens to us.

The knowledge that Krishna is now teaching he calls *Raja-vidya*, "king of knowledge." This is because his teachings summarize all Vedic philosophies and are the essence of all wisdom. In particular, the king of knowledge deals with the inner nature of the soul and the soul's life and activities beyond the body. Some think that the soul, once liberated from the body, enters a state of passive oneness. Yet here Krishna describes this inner wisdom as eternally practiced: if the soul is eternal, then the soul is active eternally, and the activities of the spiritual reality are this most secret wisdom.

KRISHNA IS WITHIN AND BEYOND EVERYTHING

4   *I pervade this universe in my hidden form. All beings are in me, but I am not in them.*

5   *Yet all beings do not rest in me. Behold my mystic opulence: supporting all yet beyond all, my Self is the source of everything.*

6   *See how the mighty wind, blowing everywhere, moves always within the vastness of space. So all beings move in me.*

7   *When one cycle ends, all beings enter my nature, and at the start of the next cycle I send them forth again.*

8   *Through my material energies, I again and again send forth this host of beings, who are helpless in nature's embrace.*

ABOVE AS WE FREELY OPEN OURSELVES TO LIFE, WE OPEN OURSELVES TO THE EMBRACE OF GOD.

9   *This work has no hold over me. I sit apart, detached from all this activity.*

10   *By my direction, nature produces all moving and nonmoving beings, and so the world revolves.*

This is the start of the confidential lesson: Krishna is present everywhere, yet at the same time he is separate. This paradox is summarized by philosophers in the phrase "inconceivable simultaneous oneness and difference." God is everywhere and we all live within him. Yet Krishna is also beyond this world, untouched by the work of creation and maintenance. He is far away in the sense that he is detached and does not interfere. Living beings have their desires, and at the beginning of each new cycle of creation he empowers them to go forth into the universal dawn to fulfill them.

Krishna does not interfere in our freedom because he is generous and his nature is unlimited. He perfectly maintains this world, and still enjoys his own separate existence. Krishna pervades the world, as the sun spreads its warmth and light, and is at the same time far away, as the sun is far away in the heavens. We can know Krishna partially by observing his material energies, but we come to know him more by thinking of him and becoming Krishna conscious. He has his personal existence and personal abode, and being the most loving person he reveals his personal existence to those who love him.

GREAT SOULS WORSHIP KRISHNA

11   *The bewildered do not recognize me when I descend in human form. They do not know my transcendent nature as the Lord of all beings.*

12   *The hopes, work, and knowledge of such misguided souls are all in vain, and their deluded nature attracts them to selfish and destructive ways.*

13   *Great souls seek the shelter of my divine nature. They know me as the inexhaustible origin of all beings, and serve me with single-minded devotion.*

14   *Always chanting my glories, endeavoring with great determination, bowing down before me, these great souls perpetually worship me with devotion.*

ABOVE KRISHNA CAME TO EARTH, WITH HIS ETERNAL COMPANION RADHA, TO REVEAL HIMSELF TO HIS DEVOTEES .

When Krishna descends to earth, he reveals his personal form and existence. Not everyone understands or believes that Krishna has an eternal personal form, and some dismiss this form as imaginary. But unless we acknowledge that God can have a personal form and existence, we see only half of reality. For the forms and personalities of this world all have their origins in the Supreme Godhead, whose form and personality surpass all beauty.

A God who merely creates and maintains the material world, and rewards or punishes its inhabitants, gives us every reason to obey his divine power, but little reason to love him. Krishna, however, as Supreme Godhead, does not want our forced obedience. He wants us freely to choose to love him. The great souls, called *mahatmas*, mentioned here as always devoted to Krishna, have understood that he is a loving person who wants our love and also wants to return it. The most confidential knowledge of the *Bhagavad Gita* is that Krishna eternally enjoys loving relationships with his spiritual companions, in a place beyond birth and death, and invites us to join him there.

We are urged therefore to glorify Krishna continuously. The essence of all religions, the constant glorification of God, is not just a formula for liturgical worship—it means a continuing awareness of the unlimited grace of God working in our lives to bring us to him. It requires that we have that mood of trust and open-heartedness already spoken of, that we always look for the loving hand of God in everything, even in life's difficulties, and that we praise him, thank him, and love him for being there. This attitude of mind can turn every act into an act of service to God. This is the meaning of the Sanskrit word *bhakti*: "devotion in action" or, as my teacher called it, "devotional service."

KRISHNA IS ALL

15   *Others, pursuing knowledge, worship me as the One, in the many, or in the Cosmic Person.*

16   *I am the ritual. I am the sacrifice and the sacred gift. I am the healing herb and the holy chant. I am the butter, the fire, and the offering into the fire.*

17   *I am father of the universe, mother, support, and grandfather. I am what is to be known, the purifier, and the syllable Om. I am the Vedic hymns:* Rig, Sama, *and* Yajur.

18   *I am goal, sustainer, master, witness, abode, refuge, and most dear friend. I am origin, dissolution, and foundation, the resting place and the eternal seed.*

19   *O Arjuna, I give heat and rain, and I withhold rain. I am immortality, and I am death. Being and nonbeing are in me.*

Here are some of the ways Krishna can be worshiped indirectly. The worshipers of God as the One are monists who worship the self in all as one with God; the worshipers of God in the many worship the gods of the universe such as the sun, moon, and fire, as forms of the one God; and the worshipers of God in the Cosmic Form worship the entire universe as a form of God. For these last devotees,

Krishna describes some of the ways that he can be experienced in the world.

These ways of experiencing God in the world allow us always to remember him. For example, we can experience the care and love of every mother for her child as a manifestation of Krishna. We usually call Krishna He, but he can also be She, the mother. His female counterpart, Radha, personifies his mercy and love. Wherever he is, she is also. Without her Krishna does nothing, and he is controlled by her love.

The rains are given by Krishna. Yet he also withholds them, and drought may be the result. Why should God withhold the most basic necessity of life in the present day when people lack rain and fresh water in many parts of the world? Rains depend on the wheel of sacrifice. If society lives in accord with nature's laws, we will have abundance, but if we take from nature without giving back, we must accept nature's consequences.

ABOVE A MOTHER'S LOVE AND CARE FOR HER CHILD ARE MANIFESTATIONS OF KRISHNA'S LOVE FOR US ALL.

CHAPTER 9

THE FRUIT OF DEVOTION

20   *Those who study the* Vedas *and drink soma juice worship me indirectly, seeking heavenly realms. Released from past sinful actions, they earn merit and reach Indra's heaven where they enjoy godly delights.*

21   *After abundant heavenly pleasures their merits are exhausted and they return to this mortal world. Seeking pleasure by following the* Vedas, *they remain in the world of birth and death.*

22   *For those who worship me with devotion, meditating on me alone, I bring what they need, and preserve what they have.*

23   *Those devoted to other gods, who worship them with faith, worship me without full understanding.*

24   *They are unaware that I am the Lord and enjoyer of all sacrifice; therefore they fall.*

25   *The worshipers of the gods are born among the gods; worshipers of ancestors go to their ancestors; spirit worshipers join the spirits; and those who worship me come to me.*

No faithfully practiced religion is decried in the *Bhagavad Gita*, which is broad in its acceptance of all paths of faith. Krishna accepts all worship offered in good faith as indirect worship of himself.

Those who worship the powers of this world, in whatever form, can expect benefits, but these rewards do not last forever. The worshiper eventually falls—that is, is reborn on earth in the cycle of birth and death.

Krishna promises to look after his devotees' welfare, materially and spiritually. No one need fear that by giving up material security to worship Krishna they will be lacking. Krishna will protect and maintain his devotees in such a way as to increase their faith in him.

GIVE EVERYTHING TO KRISHNA

26   *If one offers me with love and devotion a leaf, a flower, fruit, or water, I will accept it.*

27   *Whatever you do, eat, offer, or give away, and whatever hardship you suffer—offer it to me.*

28   *Absorbed in this yoga of renunciation, you will be released from the bondage of actions and their results, pleasant or painful. Liberated, you will come to me.*

To please Krishna is simple, because he will accept even a little water, if offered in devotion. On the basis of this revelation, devotees offer what they eat to Krishna. Food prepared from vegetables, grains, fruits, and dairy products can be offered before a picture of Krishna, with prayers for him to accept such a humble offering. The food is thus spiritualized as *prasadam*, "the mercy of God."

Krishna encourages us to make all our eating an expression of love for God—to make any act, even our struggles, an act of devotion. Life's difficulties are opportunities to remember God. It is easy to thank him for the good times, but the thanks we give him in the hard times, the struggles we offer him, are what show our faith and trust.

Life lived in this way frees us from *karma*. The cycle of *karma* is like a fruit-bearing tree representing actions, which bear bitter or sweet fruits, experienced by us as reactions. These fruits in turn bear seeds, which lie dormant in our hearts as desires, waiting to grow into new trees of action. This unending cycle of karmic reaction is dissolved by daily devotion to the Lord. This means to work for Krishna, or to think and plan how to serve the Lord. This devotional service is so powerful that a single act of service can purify the heart, and so the truth is revealed.

A DEVOTEE NEVER PERISHES

29   *I am equal to all: I reject none and I favor none. But those who serve me with devotion live in me, and I live in them.*

30   *Even one whose behavior is deeply harmful, but who serves me with faithful devotion, should be accepted as a worthy person of right intention.*

31   *This soul very soon becomes righteous and attains lasting peace. Arjuna, boldly declare, "My devotee never perishes."*

32   *All those who seek my shelter, whatever their birth, gender, caste, or status, attain the supreme destination.*

33   *And how much more so those upright priests and saintly rulers who are devoted to me. Therefore, having come to this temporary world of suffering, be devoted to me.*

34   *Think of me always, become my devotee, worship me, and bow down to me. Absorbed in me as your supreme goal, surely you will come to me.*

ABOVE A SINGLE FLOWER OFFERED TO KRISHNA WITH LOVE CAN DISSOLVE THE UNENDING CYCLE OF *KARMA*.

Krishna loves all people unconditionally and has no favorites. Yet his presence is more keenly felt by one who loves him, and so a personal exchange develops in which the Lord and his devotee respond to each other in loving relationship.

It has been said that God does not need to forgive anyone, because he is not offended in the first place. No matter how a soul behaves God loves each one, as a parent loves a child whatever a child may do. His acceptance is so complete that he helps us even when our acts are selfish. As rewarder of sacrifices in each person's heart he has promised to fulfill our desires, and does so without prejudice. God's love is reason enough for us to accept not just those who serve him with devotion, but any child of his, without condemnation.

No one is barred from devotion to Krishna, and no hard and fast rules are demanded. The yoga principles set out a clear path of behavior, but still a devotee may accidentally stray, or be compromised by the demands of material existence. However, anyone who chants Krishna's names and meditates on his form, regardless of their imperfections, is to be accepted as on the right path and worthy of love and respect. Such a devotee will soon be freed from all unwanted things and will attain him in the end.

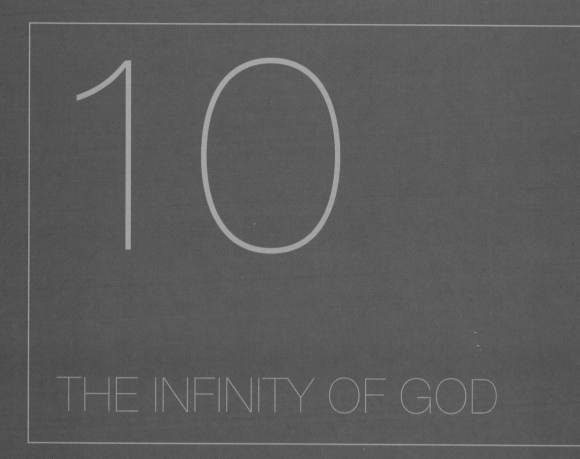

10

THE INFINITY OF GOD

Krishna reveals himself as the origin of all, who
drives away darkness from the hearts of his
devotees and fills them with divine wisdom.
Arjuna wishes to know how the Blessed One
can be perceived in this world, and in reply
Krishna sings the poem of his infinite forms.

KRISHNA'S SUPREME NATURE

The Blessed Lord said:

1   *Listen further, my beloved, as I speak still higher
     knowledge for your benefit.*

2   *The gods and great sages do not know my origin,
     for I am the source of them all.*

3   *Whoever knows me as the unborn and beginningless
     Lord of all the worlds is undeluded among mortals
     and released from all sins.*

4–5 *Intelligence, knowledge, freedom from delusion,
     forgiveness, truthfulness, self-control, calmness,
     happiness, sorrow, birth, death, fear, fearlessness,
     nonviolence, equanimity, satisfaction, austerity,
     generosity, reputation, and shame—these ways
     of being come from me alone.*

6   *The four great enlightened ones, and the seven, along
     with the Manus, are born from my mind and share my
     nature. From them all creatures are descended.*

7   *One who truly knows this opulence and power
     of mine is certain to find full absorption in yoga.*

Krishna reveals secrets hidden even from the gods to those
who, like Arjuna, accept and return his love. These secrets can
release us from our sins, that is, from the chain of action and
reaction that unfolds from our past. This is possible because
the force that binds us to our sins is not the condemnation
of God, but our own attachment. We consider ourselves the
cause of our own actions and that attachment binds us and
blinds us. We do not see that our experiences are gifts of the
Creator. Here Krishna claims the good and the bad that we see
in ourselves—our happiness and generosity as well as our fear
and shame—as states of being manifested by him in response
to our desires. When in our hearts we know the Lord of worlds
as creator of our experiences and weaver of our dreams, we
awaken from delusion and are relieved of the weight of *karma*.

The Vedic account of creation begins with the birth of
Lord Brahma, the first created being. The beings listed in the
sixth verse are born directly from Brahma: the seven great
sages who propounded the Vedic teachings; the four child
sages known as the Kumara brothers, who do perpetual
penance for the welfare of the universe; and the fourteen
Manus who are the fathers of the human race.

THE HEART OF THE *BHAGAVAD GITA*

8   *I am the source of all. Everything emanates from me. The wise who know this serve me with all their hearts.*

9   *With minds absorbed in me and lives surrendered to me, they enlighten one another and find deep satisfaction in speaking of me always, tasting transcendental bliss.*

10   *To those always absorbed in serving me with love, I give the understanding that leads to me.*

11   *Out of compassion for them, dwelling in their hearts, I destroy with the shining lamp of knowledge the darkness born of ignorance.*

These four verses form the heart of the *Bhagavad Gita*. Once the spiritual seeker has accepted Krishna as the source of all, faith and devotion naturally follow. Faith is nurtured in the company of Krishna's devotees, who find pleasure in discussing Krishna and his spiritual truths, deepening their understanding and satisfying their souls. A devotee, with deepening faith, offers service to Krishna in body and mind, and receives inner revelation through which Krishna bestows *buddhi*—knowledge of our own personal loving relationship with him. By the Lord's grace, all of the obstacles are removed from the heart of the devotee who serves him.

Devotional service to Krishna is like a seed sown in the heart by the mercy of a devotee of Krishna. The seed is watered by regular hearing and chanting of Krishna's names. The plant of devotional service grows until it pierces the coverings of the material universe and enters the spiritual sky. There it penetrates through the *brahmajyoti*, the dazzling spiritual effulgence, to find shelter in Goloka Vrindavan, the abode of Krishna, where it produces fruits and flowers at Krishna's feet. In this stage of devotion a devotee is absorbed in hearing and chanting about Krishna at every moment.

LEFT THROUGH OFFERING OURSELVES TO KRISHNA WITH LOVE, WE RECEIVE THE UNDERSTANDING THAT LEADS TO HIM.

ABOVE RIGHT KRISHNA DRIVES AWAY THE DARKNESS IN OUR HEARTS WITH THE SHINING LAMP OF KNOWLEDGE.

ARJUNA'S PRAISE

Arjuna said:

12   *You are the supreme* Brahman, *the supreme abode, and the supreme purifier. You are the eternal original divine person, unborn and greatest.*

13   *All sages say this of you, such as Narada, Asita, Devala, and Vyasa, and now you yourself are telling me.*

14   *I fully accept these truths you have given me, Krishna. Neither the gods nor demons understand your revelation.*

15   *You know yourself by your own power, O Supreme Person, Lord and Creator of all beings, God of gods, Lord of the universe.*

In the preceding verses Krishna delivers the essence of his message, offering himself in love to those who love him. Now Arjuna responds with his own affirmation, and he advances names of great Vedic teachers who have accepted Krishna's divinity.

The Vedic tradition carries spiritual authority in Asia, as have the wisdom traditions of the classical and biblical worlds in Europe. In the twenty-first century the teachings of East and West should be understood as complementary parts of a search for the divine shared by all peoples of the globe. If our human family is to find unity and peace, and a sustainable global society, we must weave their strands into a single rich tapestry.

INFINITE FORMS OF GOD

16 *Please tell me in detail of your divine powers by which you pervade all these worlds.*

17 *How shall I know you, Supreme Mystic, and always remember you? In what forms can you be contemplated, Blessed One?*

18 *Tell me again of your mystic opulences, for I never tire of hearing your sweet words.*

The Blessed Lord said:

19 *Yes, I will tell you my divine manifestations, the ones that are prominent—for my expansions are infinite.*

20 *I am the Self, seated in the hearts of all living entities. I am the beginning, middle, and end of all beings.*

21 *Of celestial deities I am Vishnu, of lights I am the radiant sun, of wind spirits I am Marichi, and among stars I am the moon.*

22 *Of Vedas I am the Sama Veda, of gods I am Indra, of senses I am the mind, and in living beings I am consciousness.*

23 *Of Rudras I am Shiva, of Yakshas and Rakshasas I am the lord of wealth, Kuvera, of Vasus I am the fire god, Agni, and of mountains I am Meru.*

24 *Of priests I am their chief, Brihaspati, of generals I am Skanda, god of war, and of bodies of water I am the ocean.*

25 *Of sages I am Bhrigu, of vibrations I am the syllable Om, of sacrifices I am Japa, and of immovable things I am the Himalayas, abodes of snow.*

26 *Of trees I am the peepal, of divine sages I am Narada, of the celestial singers I am Chitraratha, and among perfected beings I am the sage Kapila.*

27 *Of horses I am Uccaihsrava, born of nectar, of lordly elephants I am Airavata, and among men I am the monarch.*

28 *Of weapons I am the thunderbolt, of cows I am the giver of abundant milk, of progenitors I am the god of love, and among serpents I am Vasuki.*

29 *Of celestial snakes I am Ananta, of aquatics I am Varuna, of ancestors I am Aryama, and among rulers I am Yama, lord of death.*

30   Among demons I am the devoted Prahlada, of
      subduers I am time, of beasts I am the lion, and
      among birds I am Garuda.

31   Of purifiers I am the wind, of wielders of weapons
      I am Rama, of fish I am the shark, and among rivers
      I am the Ganges.

32   Of creations I am the beginning, middle, and end,
      in education I am knowledge of the self, and in
      argument I am the natural conclusion.

33   Of letters I am the vowel "A", and among compound
      words I am the dual word. I am inexhaustible time,
      and among creators I am Brahma, whose many faces
      turn everywhere.

34   I am all-devouring death and I am the source of all
      yet to be. Among women I am fame, fortune, speech,
      memory, intelligence, firmness, and patience.

35   Of hymns I am the Brhat-sama, of meters I am Gayatri,
      of months I am Magasirsha, month of harvest, and of
      seasons I am flower-bearing spring.

36   I am the gambling of cheats and the splendor of the
      splendid. I am victory, I am adventure, and I am the
      strength of the strong.

37   Of descendants of Vrishni I am Vasudeva, and of sons
      of Pandu I am Arjuna. Of the learned I am Vyasa, and
      among great thinkers I am Usana.

38   Among law enforcers I am the rod, among seekers
      of victory I am morality, of secret things I am silence,
      and among the wise I am wisdom.

39   I am the generating seed of all beings. No being,
      moving or still, exists without me.

40   There is no end to my divine manifestations.
      These I have described give only an indication
      of my infinite opulences.

ABOVE THE SACRED PEEPAL TREE GROWS IN MANY TEMPLE COMPOUNDS
IN INDIA.

41   Know that all powerful, beautiful, and glorious
      creations spring from but a spark of my splendor.

42   What need is there, Arjuna, for all these details? With
      a single fragment of myself I pervade and support
      this entire universe.

This poem of the Universal Form gives us only an idea of
Krishna's glories. If we examine any part of his creation we
will find his wonders. As words carry the poet's thoughts,
or music the mind of the composer, so the manifestations
of nature in their endless variety, from smallest to greatest,
display the infinite shades of colors, thoughts, energies,
emotions, and graces of Krishna, the Supreme Artist.

Japa is a widely practiced method of prayer or meditation.
A chosen mantra, usually including names of God, is
repeated softly or silently while counting on a string
of 108 beads called a Mala.

The peepal tree, whose Sanskrit name is asvattha,
is the most revered and long-lived of the fig family, which
includes the banyan tree. Peepal and banyan trees are
planted to give shelter to Hindu shrines. The peepal tree is
also sacred to Buddhists because under it Gautama Buddha
achieved enlightenment.

11

VISION OF THE UNIVERSAL FORM

Given divine eyes, Arjuna sees all time and space in the awesome display of Krishna's Universal Form. He sees the soldiers on the battlefield destroyed like moths in a flame. Filled with fear, he longs to see Krishna's gentle form of love.

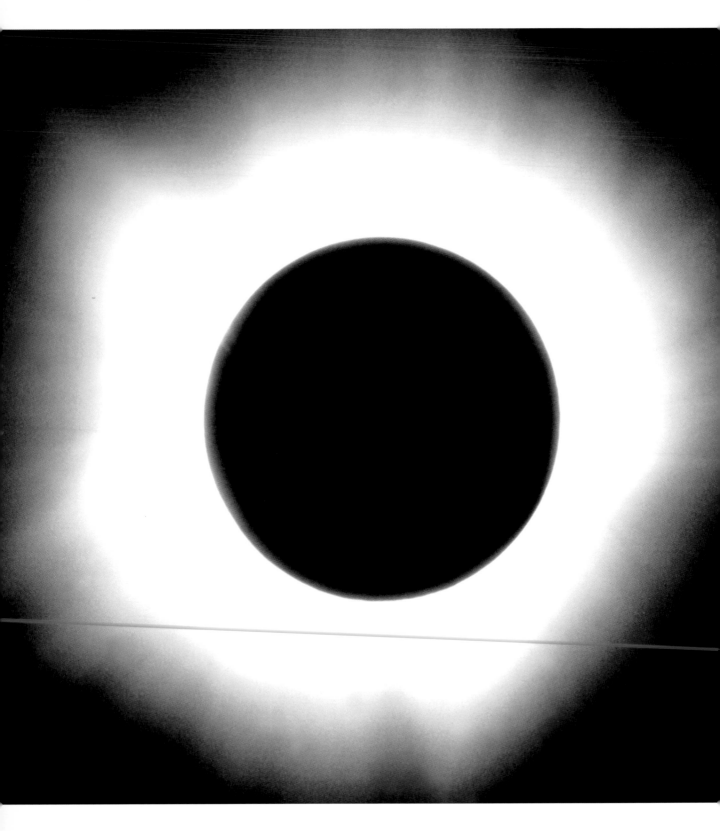

ARJUNA WISHES FOR DIVINE EYES

Arjuna said:

1   *You have favored me with this innermost spiritual secret, and your words have dispelled my illusion.*

2   *Lotus-eyed One, you have told me everything of the origin and destiny of living beings and your inexhaustible greatness.*

3   *As you have said, Lord, so you are. O Supreme Person, I wish to see your form of majesty.*

4   *If you think I have the eyes to see, Lord of mystic powers, show me your cosmic Self.*

The Blessed Lord said:

5   *Behold, Arjuna, my hundreds of thousands of divine forms, infinite in color and shape.*

6   *See here the Adityas, Vasus, Rudras, Asvins, Maruts, and many wonders never before revealed.*

7   *See at once the entire universe, with all creatures moving and still, and whatever else you desire, here in my body.*

8   *But you cannot see me with your present eyes, so I give you divine eyes. Behold now my mystic opulence!*

After hearing of Krishna's infinite energies Arjuna is convinced that Krishna is the supreme source of everything. Now, for the benefit of others, he wants Krishna to demonstrate his divinity. People naturally want to see for themselves the secret of how God enters and supports the cosmos, and they try through scientific research to penetrate

the mysteries of reality. Such revelations, however, remain hidden, for the human mind does not have the capacity to receive them. Whatever we conceive will be subjective and flawed. Even if we could somehow achieve unbounded vision, it would be bewildering and intolerable, as Arjuna is about to discover. The mind capable of holding such a universal vision is the mind of God.

KRISHNA REVEALS HIS UNIVERSAL FORM

Sanjaya said:

9   *So saying, the Personality of Godhead, Supreme Lord of mystic power, revealed to Arjuna his Universal Form.*

10–11   *Arjuna saw numberless wonderful forms with countless mouths and eyes, clothed in celestial robes and garlands, adorned with divine ornaments and perfumes, and bearing many raised weapons. All was wondrous, effulgent, infinite, and all-expanding.*

12   *If a thousand suns were to rise at once in the sky, their brilliance might equal the radiance of that Supreme Person.*

13   *In the body of the Lord of lords Arjuna saw the unlimited aspects of the universe united in one place.*

14   *Full of wonder, his hair on end, Arjuna bowed his head before the Lord and prayed with folded hands.*

Arjuna's vision of the Universal Form is one of the great mystical passages of world literature. It captures the majesty of the cosmic reality as well as its awesome power, as much as can be communicated in words. There is more here than poetic fancy—these words bear the authentic stamp of one who has witnessed at least a fragment of what is described.

The spiritual seeker is sometimes blessed with a moment in which the veil is lifted, momentarily allowing a glimpse of what lies beyond the appearance of normal life. These rare moments are high points on the spiritual journey, inspiring faith and conviction. Yet they cannot be sustained, for each of us, in working as we are called on to do within our subjective reality, must find in our lives the presence of God. As Krishna earlier says to Arjuna, "For one who sees me everywhere and sees everything in me, I am never lost, nor is that one ever lost to me."

LEFT THE RADIANCE OF KRISHNA'S UNIVERSAL FORM IS BRIGHTER THAN A THOUSAND SUNS.

THE AWESOME VISION

Arjuna said:

15 *I see gathered in your body, Lord, gods and beings of all kinds. I see Brahma seated on his lotus, and Shiva, and divine sages and serpents.*

16 *I see spread around me your limitless form with infinite arms, bellies, mouths, and eyes. I can see no beginning, middle, or end to this cosmic vision, Lord of the universe.*

17 *Your dazzling form, adorned with crowns, clubs, and discs, with fiery effulgence spread on every side, is hard to look upon like the sun.*

18 *You are the everlasting goal of knowledge, supreme shelter of the universe, enduring guardian of truth, and the eternal Personality of Godhead. This is my conviction.*

19 *You have no beginning, middle, or end. Your arms are numberless and the sun and moon are your eyes. Flames, blazing from your mouths, consume the universe.*

20 *The three worlds tremble, O Great One, to see your wonderful and terrible form that fills all space between heaven and earth.*

21 *Hosts of gods enter you, some in fear, offering prayers with folded hands. Saints and sages praise you, crying "All peace!" and chant Vedic hymns.*

22 *The gods—Rudras, Adityas, Vasus, Sadhyas, Visves, Asvins, and Maruts—along with forefathers, angels, spirits, demons, and all perfected beings, behold you in wonder.*

23 *The worlds are terrified by your vast form, with infinite faces, eyes, arms, thighs, legs, bellies, and fearsome teeth, and so am I.*

24 *Seeing you spread across the sky radiating infinite colors, with gaping mouths and great blazing eyes, my mind is lost. O Vishnu, I am afraid.*

25 *Lord of lords, refuge of the worlds, be merciful upon me. Seeing your blazing deathlike faces and mighty teeth I have lost all sense of direction and safety.*

26–27 *The sons of Dhritarashtra and their host of allies, with Bhisma, Drona, and Karna—and our heroes too—rush into your fearsome mouths. Some are caught with their heads crushed between your teeth.*

28 *As waves of a river hasten to the ocean, these great heroes enter your fiery throats.*

29 *As moths rush into the flames of a lamp so all people perish in your blazing mouths.*

30 *O Vishnu, your effulgence fills the universe and scorches all people. Thus your terrible radiance consumes all.*

31 *Lord of lords, so fierce of form, I bow before you—please be merciful and tell me who you are. I wish to know you, Ancient One, and what your mission is.*

This display of raw power fills Arjuna with fear. Fear of God is sometimes encouraged by religion because fear induces obedience. It is said that rulers of old placed in scriptures accounts of punishments in hell to frighten people into good behavior. Such forced obedience and fear may in the beginning nurture a sense of reverence and dependence on God, but it masks the true inclination of the soul. Fear must be replaced by love if the soul is to find happiness and if religion is to bring peace to the world.

THE VISION SPEAKS

The Blessed Lord said:

32 *Time I am, destroyer of the worlds, and I have come to destroy all beings. Except for you, all who enter this fight on both sides will be slain.*

33 *Rise, therefore, win glory, and after conquering your enemies enjoy the flourishing kingdom. They are already put to death by my arrangement, and you, Arjuna, can be but an instrument in the fight.*

34 *Drona, Bhisma, Jayadratha, Karna, and the other great fighters are destroyed by me. Therefore, kill them without fear. Simply fight, and you will vanquish your enemies in battle.*

Events sometimes appear ghastly, and God's will seems incomprehensible, yet we must have faith that the world moves to bring all souls to freedom and love, when they are ready. God comes at last, even to the unfaithful, in the form of death, the ultimate fear in this world. One who seeks as Arjuna does to be God's instrument, living as Krishna has asked with detachment and compassion for others, has nothing to fear in life or in death.

ABOVE THE AWESOME UNIVERSAL FORM OF GOD INSPIRES OUR REVERENCE AND OUR FEAR.

ARJUNA'S PRAYERS

Sanjaya said:

35   *Trembling with fear while hearing these words, with head bowed and hands folded, Arjuna spoke to Lord Krishna in faltering voice.*

Arjuna said:

36   *The world becomes joyful on hearing your name, Krishna, and all are attracted to you. While perfect ones revere you, demons fly from you in fear.*

37   *And why should they not revere you, Great One? you are the infinite God of gods, original creator even of Brahma, and shelter of the universe. You are the imperishable cause of all, and yet beyond all.*

38   *You are the original Godhead, Oldest Person and highest abode of this universe. You are knower and knowable, and supreme refuge. Your limitless form pervades the cosmos.*

39   *You are air, fire, water, moon, and death, father and grandfather of all creatures. I offer my respects to you a thousand times, again and yet again!*

40   *I bow to you in front, behind, and on all sides. Unbounded power, limitless might, you are everywhere and so you are everything.*

41   *Unaware of your greatness, I have in the past called you "Krishna," "my friend," in confusion and love.*

42   *I disrespected you, joking as we relaxed alone or with many friends, lying on a bed, sitting or eating together. Infallible One, please forgive my offenses.*

43   *Father of all beings, worshiped by all as supreme teacher, no one in the three worlds can equal or surpass you, for your glory is beyond measure.*

44   *I fall to the ground imploring your mercy, worshipful Lord. As a father with his son, as a friend with a friend, or a lover with his beloved, be patient with me.*

45   *I see what has never been seen before and I am grateful, yet my mind is full of fear. Please, therefore, show me your own form and be kind to me, Lord of lords, refuge of the universe.*

46   *O thousand-armed Cosmic Lord, I long to see your four-handed form, with helmet on your head, and club and discus in your hands.*

Krishna has revealed to Arjuna that he will be successful in the battle, so he is joyful now, with nothing to fear. However, those who act with hatred for others fear the power of God because they fear the consequences of their actions. They do not want to open their hearts, to God or to anyone, for fear of exposure and rejection. Thus they fear the very idea of God, from whom there can be no secrets. This fear is groundless, because God is merciful and is the shelter of all, even of those who have adopted the nature of demons.

Arjuna reminds Krishna of their personal friendship. This is more important to him than the display of Krishna's power as lord of the three worlds (the heavens, the earth, and the lower realms). Krishna's love for his devotees, as father and son, as friends, or as lover and beloved, is revealed in Krishna's play on earth. In such relationships, Krishna's power and divinity is entirely forgotten in the presence of love.

LEFT KRISHNA'S ETERNAL LOVE FOR HIS CREATION IS REVEALED IN HIS *RASAMANDALA* CIRCLE DANCE WITH THE COWHERD GIRLS OF VRINDAVAN.

SEEING WITH THE EYES OF LOVE

The Blessed Lord said:

47   *Dear Arjuna, I am glad to show you this supreme*
     form through my mystic power. No one before you
     has seen this primal, infinite, and dazzling vision.

48   *This cannot be seen by study of the Vedas, sacrifice,*
     charity, pious works, or severe penances. You are the
     only one in this world to have seen this.

49   *You have been troubled and bewildered by this*
     frightening aspect of mine. Now let it be finished. With
     peaceful heart and without fears, see my own form.

Sanjaya said:

50   *So saying, Krishna showed his four-armed form.*
     Encouraging the fearful Arjuna, the Great One then
     resumed his gentle and most beautiful appearance.

Arjuna said:

51   *Krishna, seeing your humanlike form, so gentle,*
     my mind is pacified and I am restored to my
     original nature.

The Blessed Lord said:

52   *This form of mine seen by you is very difficult to*
     behold. The gods always long to see this form.

53   *This form is not revealed through study of the Vedas,*
     penance, charity, or worship.

54   *Dear Arjuna, you can know and see me as I am, here*
     before you, only by undivided devotional service, and
     so enter the mysteries of my existence.

55   *One who works for me in devotion, depending on me*
     without worldly attachments, friendly to all beings,
     comes to me.

Krishna's most intimate form is called here *saumyam*,
meaning "gentle and beautiful." This form is unlike the
majestic and frightening Universal Form, for it is manifested
for his loving relationships with his devotees. Krishna's four-
handed form, requested by Arjuna, is his form of opulence as

ABOVE KRISHNA LIVED IN THE FOREST HERDING COWS AND PLAYING
HIS FLUTE.

Narayana, worshiped and served in reverence. After showing
this Narayana form he returned to his original humanlike
appearance as Govinda. This original form is the source of
all others and can be seen and understood by those who
serve Krishna in devotion, giving up worldly association and
showing love to others. Krishna with two hands playing the
flute, dancing with his companions in the forest of Vrindavan,
is the most intimate vision of God. To see this form of
Krishna is truly to enter the mysteries of his existence.

12

THE WAY
OF DEVOTION

Two paths lead to Krishna: the path of
personal devotion and the path of impersonal
meditation. Krishna recommends the path of
personal devotion as the easiest and most
direct, and describes the qualities of those
who are dear to him.

SERVICE OR MEDITATION?

Arjuna said:

1   *Of those who always serve you in devotion, and
     those who contemplate the Imperishable and
     Imperceptible—who are the most perfect in yoga?*

The Blessed Lord said:

2   *Those whose minds are focused on me, who are
     absorbed in my constant service with great faith,
     I consider the most perfect yogis.*

3–4   *But those who contemplate the Imperceptible—
     invisible, all-pervading, inconceivable, unchanging,
     fixed, and immovable—by controlling all the senses
     and being even-minded, living for the welfare of all,
     they also attain me.*

5   *Yet their trouble is great, for the path to the
     imperceptible is difficult for mortals to follow.*

6–7   *Those who dedicate all their actions to me—who
     are attached to me and absorbed in yoga, who
     remember and worship me, whose minds are fixed on
     me—I soon deliver from the ocean of birth and death.*

There are two spiritual paths followed by practitioners of
yoga: some are attracted to the path of devotional service
and some to the path of impersonal contemplation.
Ultimately both paths reach the same goal, but Krishna
says at the end of the sixth chapter that one who faithfully
serves him with devotion is the greatest yogi. Now Arjuna
asks about those who are attracted to the all-pervading
impersonal aspect of God.

Having witnessed the display of Krishna's inconceivable
energies, Arjuna needs to be reassured that he really will be
able to enter into a personal, devotional relationship with
this Universal Lord. Is such a personal relationship real,
or is it better to follow the other path—to contemplate the
impersonal Oneness?

Krishna here makes the clearest distinction between
the two paths: the path of personal devotion, *bhakti* yoga,
is direct and most perfect; the path of abstract meditation,
jnana yoga, also leads to perfection, but is difficult and
troublesome. One path depends on the grace of the Lord
and the other on the determination of the follower. Krishna's
advice is clear: follow the path of devotion.

RIGHT WE GAIN STRENGTH IN SPIRITUAL LIFE BY HEARING AND CHANTING
IN THE ASSOCIATION OF DEVOTEES.

BELOW THE STAGES OF DEVOTIONAL LIFE LEAD US ON, STEP BY STEP,
INTO THE PERSONAL PRESENCE OF KRISHNA

STAGES ON THE PATH

8   *Fix your mind on me, absorb your intelligence in me.*
       Thus you will live in me always, without a doubt.

9   *If you cannot fix your mind upon me without deviation,*
       then try to reach me by regular practice of yoga.

10   *If you cannot do this regular practice, then devote*
       yourself to working for me, for just by working for
       my sake you will achieve perfection.

11   *If you are unable to work under my shelter, then*
       control your mind and work without attachment
       to the fruits of your actions.

12   *Knowledge is better than practice, meditation is*
       better than knowledge, and giving up the fruits of
       action is better than meditation, for from detachment
       comes peace.

Here are the stages of devotional practice in descending order. The most perfect is full absorption in spontaneous love for Krishna, through which every act merges into transcendence. The way to achieve this consciousness is to follow the principles of *bhakti* yoga, under the guidance of a teacher, purifying one's senses in the service of Krishna, beginning with hearing and chanting his names, associating with his devotees, and remembering him, and thus awakening one's dormant love of God. Before this, one can offer service to Krishna by supporting his work and the work of his devotees, or one can devote oneself to Krishna in any occupation, and at the same time chant, *Hare Krishna Hare Krishna Krishna Krishna Hare Hare, Hare Rama Hare Rama Rama Rama Hare Hare*, and reach perfection. If none of these methods is possible, one can practice *karma* yoga, giving up the results of one's work for the welfare of others, and ultimately for the Supreme.

For those not attracted to the path of devotional service, the Lord lastly summarizes the impersonal path that leads from action to knowledge, to inner absorption, to detachment, and finally to peace and liberation from material life.

THE ONE WHO IS DEAR TO THE LORD

13   One who bears no hatred, who is a compassionate
      friend to all creatures, who is not possessive or
      selfish, equal in happiness and distress, and forgiving,

14   Who is dedicated to the spiritual path, always
      satisfied, self-controlled, and determined, whose
      mind and intelligence are fixed on me—this devotee
      of mine is dear to me.

15   One who troubles no one and is troubled by no one,
      who is unmoved by happiness, anger, fear, or
      distress—is dear to me.

16   One who is detached, pure, skillful, without cares or
      troubles, and selfless in all endeavors—this devotee
      of mine is dear to me.

17   One who does not grasp joy or hatred, grief or desire,
      good or bad—this devoted soul is dear to me.

18–19 One who looks equally on friends or enemies, honor
      or dishonor, heat or cold, happiness or distress,
      praise or blame, who craves nothing, is silent and
      satisfied in any situation, who has no home, who is
      even-minded and filled with devotion—such a person
      is dear to me.

20   Those who faithfully follow this eternal path of
      devotion, making me their Supreme Goal, are dearly
      beloved to me.

The qualities of one devoted to the Lord are the inner
qualities of the soul, revealed as the spirit is progressively
freed from the coverings of material ego. Such qualities are
naturally attractive to the Lord. A devotee of Krishna accepts
distress as a just consequence of distress given to others,
and as an opportunity to learn and purify the heart—by the
Lord's mercy this distress is kept to a minimum, and so the
devotee is calm and quiet despite all difficulties. A devotee
is kind to all creatures, even to those who consider
themselves enemies, because the devotee identifies with
the spirit, not the body. To be silent means to speak only
the truth about Krishna and the spirit. To have no home
means to feel equally at home under the sky or in a
comfortable residence.

The theme underlying all these qualities is one of
detachment and acceptance, and ultimately of surrender
to the will of the Lord. It is said that there are six aspects of
surrender to Krishna:

1. to accept all that is favorable to the Lord's service
2. to avoid all that is unfavorable to the Lord's service
3. to have full faith in the Lord as protector
4. to have confidence in the Lord as maintainer
5. to be dependent on the will of the Lord
6. to be always humble before the Lord

On the path of surrender to Krishna one feels increasing
joy. Therefore it is here described by the Lord as *amrita*, "full
of nectar." To have faith on the path of devotional service
means to believe that simply by offering service to Krishna
all other needs will be taken care of, and the benefits that
arise from all other paths—whether by penance, sacrifice,
religious ritual, obedience, morality, duty, or study—will be
fulfilled by making Krishna the supreme goal of life.

The conclusion of the twelfth chapter is that the path
of mystic meditation on the impersonal aspect of God is
recommended so long as one's love for Krishna is dormant.
If by good fortune the soul hears about the Personality of
Godhead from a devotee of Krishna, love of God will awaken.
Then the path of devotional service is open, and the devoted
soul is soon rescued from the ocean of birth and death.

ABOVE LEFT A LOVER OF GOD FEELS EQUALLY SECURE UNDER THE SKY OR
AT HOME SURROUNDED BY THEIR FAMILY.

RIGHT JOY IS THE NATURE OF THE SOUL, AND SHINES FORTH AS WE FOLLOW
THE SPIRITUAL PATH.

13

NATURE AND
THE SOUL

The soul labors in the field of this world, harvesting the fruits of happiness and distress. To distinguish between the field and the soul, between matter and spirit, is true wisdom. Such wisdom is a gift of the Supersoul, who makes all things possible.

THE FIELD OF ACTION

*   *Krishna, I wish to know of nature and the soul, of
the field of action and the knower of the field, and
of knowledge and the end of knowledge.*

The Blessed Lord said:

1   *This body is the field, and the one conscious of it is
the knower of the field. So it is said by the wise.*

2   *I am also the knower of the field in all bodies. To
understand this field and its knower I regard as
true wisdom.*

3   *Hear from me in brief about the nature of the field,
its source and forms, and about the one who knows
and influences it.*

4   *Sages have sung of this in various ways in the Vedic
hymns, and analyzed its causes and effects in such
writings as the Brahma Sutras.*

5–6   *These, in essence, make up the field and its forms:
the five physical elements, ego, intellect, the total
material substance, the eleven senses and organs
with the mind, the five sensory objects, desire and
hatred, pleasure and pain, the combination of all
these, consciousness and conviction.*

This world is a combination of spirit and matter. Spirit is eternal, active, and joyful, whereas the forms of matter are temporary, passive, and without feeling. When spirit and matter combine, the endless fluctuations and varieties of earthly life are produced.

The analogy of a field is given for the material body, because a field is where we labor to plant and nurture grains for the harvest, witnessed by the sun and rain. Similarly the soul, wishing to enjoy the fruits of work, labors in the field of the world amid the mind and senses, harvesting the fruits of happiness or sorrow, witnessed by the Supreme Lord. By realizing ourselves as separate from the field we are freed.

The ancient philosophy called *Sankhya* analyzes the field into the twenty-four elements summarized here. The aim of Sankhya philosophy is to distinguish the soul from these twenty-four, which include the mind, intellect, and ego. The soul is none of these, nor is it an illusion arising from interactions of molecules—it is eternal spirit distinct from matter. If we are truthfully to understand this world and the aim of life we must see the difference between matter and spirit.

THE SUM OF ALL KNOWLEDGE

7–11 *Humility, modesty, nonviolence, forgiveness, truthfulness, service to the teacher, cleanliness, steadiness, self-control, freedom from sensual desires, absence of false ego, awareness of the pain and sorrow of birth, death, old age, and disease, detachment from the comforts of family and home, even-mindedness amid pleasant and unpleasant events, unwavering devotion to my service, attraction to secluded places, aversion to the crowd, dedication to self-realization, and pursuit of the truth—these are said to make up knowledge, and their contrary is ignorance.*

The foundation of knowledge is the realization that the soul is different from the body. One who lives in the awareness of being a spirit in the material world will naturally incline toward humility, respect for all beings, and detachment from material life. The more we understand, the less we find we know, and thus the first sign of knowledge is humility. In time such understanding leads the wise to surrender themselves to the Supreme Lord, the end of knowledge, described in the following verses.

THE END OF KNOWLEDGE

12 *I will tell you the end of knowledge, by which you will taste eternity. This is called the beginningless Brahman, which emanates from me and lies beyond the cause and effect of this world.*

13 *Everywhere are his hands and legs, his eyes and faces, and he hears everything. In this way he covers the world.*

14 *He is the source of the senses, yet without senses. He is unattached and yet maintains all. He transcends the qualities of nature, and yet enjoys them.*

15 *He exists within and outside all beings, moving and still. He is far away, beyond the perception of the senses, yet very near.*

16 *He appears divided among all beings, yet exists as one. He, the creator, maintainer, and dissolver of all, is the end of knowledge.*

17 *He is the light in all that shines, beyond the darkness of matter. He is knowledge, the end of knowledge, and the goal of knowledge. He dwells in everyone's heart.*

18 *This summarizes the field of activities, knowledge, and the end of knowledge. My devotee who understands this attains my nature.*

The individual soul and the Supreme Soul are described as the end of knowledge, the final truth. Both are *Brahman*, or spirit. The Supreme Soul, expanded as one soul inhabiting all bodies, is called in Sanskrit the *Paramatma* (Supersoul), while the individual soul in each body is called the *atma*. The individual soul and the Supersoul are one in quality as pure spirit, but different in quantity. The soul is described in the *Upanishads* as infinitesimally small, one ten-thousandth the size of the tip of a hair; the Supersoul is infinitely large. The soul, being small, may forget the Supersoul, but the Supersoul never forgets the soul; they are never separated.

The Supreme is described here as without material senses and qualities, but he possesses spiritual senses and qualities. He is the source of the senses and qualities of this world; whatever exists in this world has its origin in him.

CHAPTER 13

SOUL AND SUPERSOUL

19   *Know nature and the soul to be beginningless, and nature as the source of the forms and qualities of matter.*

20   *Nature is the cause of activities and effects, and the soul is the cause of feelings of suffering or enjoyment. So it is said.*

21   *Thus the soul, dwelling in nature, is attracted to nature's qualities, and under their influence meets with good or bad fortune in different births.*

22   *The Supreme Soul is the Witness, living in all bodies as ordainer, enjoyer, and sustainer. He is the Lord of all and is called the Supersoul.*

23   *Those who understand this teaching of the soul, nature, and the qualities of nature, regardless of their present state, will not be born again.*

The soul ever seeks enjoyment, because joy is the nature of spirit. This search leads the soul, through attraction to different qualities of nature, to be born into different wombs, fortunate or unfortunate, and to travel throughout the universe, experiencing transient happiness and distress. This process of transmigration influenced by the qualities of nature will be described later.

   The Supersoul, as ordainer and sustainer, supports the individual soul on this journey of experience and discovery, arranging for different bodies and senses to aid self-discovery and ultimately to bring the soul to true understanding. All the while, the Lord as Witness speaks to us through our inner voice of conscience and wisdom. He speaks in dreams, through the mind or intelligence, through sacred books and teachers, and through the world around us. His guidance is always there if we are open to receiving it. The Supersoul is the enjoyer because he is the inspiration behind all enjoyment. Once we recognize him as our friend we will taste the joy of the spirit, and no longer be attracted to rebirth in this world.

THE LIGHT OF WISDOM

24   *Some see the Supersoul within through meditation, others through the path of knowledge, and others through the path of action.*

25   *Some, though they do not understand, hear with faith from those who do and so worship the Lord. They too pass beyond death.*

26   *Whatever exists in this world, moving or still, Arjuna, is a combination of the field and the knower of the field.*

27   *One who sees the Supersoul dwelling equally in all beings, everlasting amid the transient, truly sees.*

28   *One who sees the Lord equally present everywhere never harms the self, and so attains the supreme goal.*

29   *One who sees that all is done by nature, while the self does nothing, truly sees.*

30   *A person who sees the multitude of separate beings expanded everywhere, all existing in the One, attains Brahman.*

31   *The transcendent self, beginningless and imperishable, is beyond material qualities. Though dwelling in the body, the self does nothing and is unaffected by matter.*

32   *The sky, though all-pervading, remains pure because it is subtle. Similarly the self, though inhabiting the body, remains untouched.*

33   *As the sun illuminates the whole world, so the self, knower of the field, illuminates the field of the body.*

34   *Those who see, by the light of wisdom, this distinction between the field and its knower, and who see the path to freedom from matter, attain the Supreme.*

By the light of spiritual wisdom we can see the Supersoul present in all beings, sustaining all and impartially witnessing their lives. With this understanding it is possible to accept all beings as they are—since the Lord himself does so—and give no harm to any creature, including to ourselves. This way lies peace.

   The soul illuminates the body with consciousness as the sun lights up the world, and as the sun is untouched by the world, so the soul is untouched by the body and its actions.

The soul does not control the body, which is controlled by nature under the direction of the Supersoul. The soul merely desires to act, and the rest is done by nature. We must therefore accept the limitations of the body we have been given, and aim our desires toward the service of the Lord.

If one cannot fully understand the meaning of this thirteenth chapter of the *Bhagavad Gita*, Krishna gives encouragement. By hearing these truths with faith from one who understands them, Krishna promises, one will still achieve liberation from the cycle of birth and death. This is an encouragement to find a spiritual teacher, which is a sure step toward spiritual success.

The *Bhagavad Gita* is a scripture of grace, inserted into the *Mahabharata*, the popular history of ancient India and intended to be heard and understood by ordinary folk who were not philosophers or renouncers of the world. Its message of grace is especially relevant in today's distracted world, where many have lost all faith in religion. Krishna's path of grace grants spiritual knowledge not by learning or good behavior, but through devotion. If, by hearing with faith, we take to the worship of God, most easily by chanting his names, we are here assured by Krishna of liberation from birth and death.

14

THREE QUALITIES OF MATERIAL NATURE

Nature is made of three qualities—goodness, passion, and darkness—which combine to produce all forms and actions. To see these qualities, to be undisturbed by their changes and interactions, and to know that Krishna lies beyond them, is to achieve spiritual freedom.

LEFT "NATURE IS THE WOMB IN WHICH I PLACE MY SEED, CAUSING THE BIRTH OF ALL CREATURES."

In this chapter Krishna, as father of us all, offers knowledge that goes farther than any he has taught so far, revealing practical information about how material nature conditions us to behave as we do. As children of Krishna and nature, we are influenced by both mother and father. Our mother's influence binds us to her and our father calls us to self-discovery. Having understood the principles taught here about the three qualities of nature, we can become conscious of how nature binds us and we can begin to change our behavior. It is the same principle as understanding how the influences received in childhood from our parents condition our adult behavior. So long as that conditioning is unconscious we are bound by it, but by recognizing it we have the option to change the way we act. Here, and in the following chapters, Krishna gives the tools for personal transformation, to enable us change our behavior from darkness and passion to goodness, and to discover our identity as pure soul.

NATURE'S THREE QUALITIES

5   *The primary qualities of goodness, passion, and darkness, arising from nature, bind the eternal soul to the body.*

6   *The quality of goodness is purity, which brings illumination and well-being. Goodness binds the self with attachment to happiness and learning.*

7   *The quality of passion is desire, born of attraction and longings. Passion binds the self with attachment to work.*

8   *But the quality of darkness is ignorance, which deludes all beings. Darkness binds the self with forgetfulness, laziness, and sleep.*

The three primary qualities of nature are called *guna*, which in Sanskrit means "rope"—goodness is *sattva guna*; passion is *raja guna*, and darkness is *tama guna*. Woven together they bind us to the world. Like the three primary colors of yellow, red, and blue, which mix to create all colors, the qualities of nature combine and interact in endless permutations. So long as we live in this world we cannot escape their primary influences—they affect all that we do.

THE FATHER OF ALL

The Blessed Lord said:

1   *I shall teach further supreme wisdom, highest of all knowledge. The sages who understood this passed from here to supreme perfection.*

2   *By taking shelter of this knowledge, one attains my own nature. Thus one is not born at the time of creation or disturbed at the time of dissolution.*

3   *Nature is the womb in which I place my seed, causing the birth of all living beings, Arjuna.*

4   *All species born into this world come from the womb of nature, with me as their seed-giving father.*

It is said that nature is impregnated by the glance of the Lord, and from her womb are born all creatures, on the land, in the air, and in the waters, on this planet and on all other planets of the universe.

HOW THE THREE INTERACT

9   *Goodness attracts one to happiness, passion to work, and darkness covers knowledge and attracts one to forgetfulness.*

10 *Sometimes goodness prevails over passion and darkness, sometimes passion dominates goodness and darkness, and sometimes darkness overwhelms goodness and passion.*

11 *When the light of understanding radiates through all the doors of the body, know that goodness prevails.*

12 *Greed, hard work, ambition, dissatisfaction, and craving arise when passion dominates.*

13 *Depression, laziness, forgetfulness, and delusion arise when darkness overwhelms.*

14 *A soul who passes from this world under the influence of goodness attains the pure realms of the enlightened.*

15 *The soul who passes away in passion is reborn among those attached to work, and one who dies in darkness is born into the animal kingdom.*

16 *The fruit of work in goodness is purity and more goodness. The fruit of passion is unhappiness, and the fruit of darkness is ignorance.*

The earthly realm is dominated by passion, which urges people to work and compete for success and power. Under the influence of passion we seek a sexual partner with whom to set up a home and gather possessions, forming the foundation for social and economic development. But passion carries a high price: under its influence we are never satisfied and always want more, and this leads to struggles for supremacy between people, communities, and nations, both in business and in war. There is enough provided by nature for all her children, but human greed creates constant competition for her precious resources. The conflicts and human misery thus engendered are the product of passion.

Goodness brings happiness and knowledge. A person influenced by this quality is peaceful and self-sufficient, preferring not to compete with those in passion. But goodness binds the soul to a false sense of satisfaction and security in an insecure world.

Darkness brings forgetfulness and delusion. Where people have lost their sense of purpose, having no respect for themselves or others, taking shelter in intoxication to deaden their minds, there is darkness. In this condition the qualities of the soul seem to be negated, so that a person may behave in a way that is destructive or cruel, even evil. This effect of the quality of darkness will be examined in the sixteenth chapter of the *Bhagavad Gita*.

BELOW THE VARIETIES OF NATURE ARE A MIXTURE OF THE THREE QUALITIES OF GOODNESS, PASSION, AND DARKNESS—JUST AS ALL COLORS COME FROM YELLOW, RED, AND BLUE.

UNDERSTANDING THE THREE

17 *From goodness is born knowledge, from passion comes greed, and darkness brings forgetfulness, delusion, and ignorance.*

18 *Those situated in goodness rise upward, those in passion stay in the middle, and those ruled by darkness, lowest of all, sink downward.*

19 *One who sees no other performer at work than these primary qualities, and knows what lies beyond them, attains my nature.*

20 *The soul who rises above these three qualities of the body is freed from birth, death, old age, and their distresses, and tastes the nectar of eternal life.*

Living beings move ceaselessly upward or downward through species and spheres of existence, and the destination we reach in the next life is a consequence of our choices in this one. Human life on earth offers freedom of moral choice: from here we can choose our future destination, either to return to this earthly realm of passion, or to rise upward. Above the earth are heavenly planes where the enlightened proceed, or where souls are rewarded for their good deeds on earth. Beneath human life are the lower species of animal and plant life. If we live human life in darkness we deny our spiritual nature, and in response to that choice the soul sinks into animal species, where the spiritual nature is covered, or into the forms of plants or trees where the soul enters deep slumber.

In the modern world the influence of passion and darkness are very strong, and as a consequence we are laying down huge problems for the future. The solution lies in cultivating the quality of goodness in all ways possible, as will be described in the remaining chapters.

TRANSCENDING THE THREE

Arjuna said:

21 *What are the signs and behavior of one who has risen above the three qualities, Lord, and how does one transcend these three?*

The Blessed Lord said:

22 *One who is not averse to illumination, hard work, or delusion when they are present, nor desires them when they are absent…*

23 *Who is detached, undisturbed by the different qualities, firm in the knowledge that the qualities alone are active…*

24 *Who is centered on the self, equal to happiness or distress, to earth, stone, or gold, to the desirable or the undesirable, to praise or blame…*

25 *Who is unaffected by honor or dishonor, neutral among friends and enemies, who gives up all selfish endeavors—such a person, Arjuna, is said to have transcended the qualities of nature.*

A wandering teacher once visited the court of a king. The king inquired of him, "How is the soul bound to this world?" In answer the wanderer tightly embraced a pillar of the king's palace while calling, "Release me!" His meaning was that the soul is bound to this world both by attachment and aversion to nature. Krishna's advice is to be neutral toward all three qualities, neither attached nor detached, accepting goodness, passion, and darkness as belonging to the tapestry of life. Goodness enlightens and brings peace, passion encourages work and creativity, darkness brings rest and forgetfulness. All have their own place in the passage of life. We should neither desire them nor abhor them, but accept all as the Lord gives it, and so be free.

FOUNDATION OF ALL

26 *One who serves me with unfailing devotion, in* bhakti *yoga, rises above these qualities of material nature and achieves the level of* Brahman.

27 *I am the basis of the immortal and imperishable* Brahman, *and the abode of everlasting truth and ultimate happiness.*

RIGHT AS WE MOVE THROUGH THE WORLD, OUR DESTINATIONS IN THIS LIFE AND THE NEXT ARE THE RESULT OF THE CHOICES WE MAKE.

Krishna answers Arjuna's final question, "How does one transcend the qualities of nature?" He has already explained that a person who is neutral toward the qualities transcends them—but how, when our nature is to be attached, do we achieve such neutrality? The answer is to give our attachment to the eternal Lord and thus become neutral toward his creation. This means that, instead of serving material nature, we endeavor to serve Krishna in *bhakti* yoga, and so become free. This surrender brings the soul to the level of *Brahman*, above the qualities of nature. On this spiritual level of *Brahman* the soul shares the same spiritual nature as the Lord, and the eternal exchange of love between the soul and God awakens, full of eternal truth and ultimate happiness.

15

THE SUPREME PERSON

The tree of this world extends in all directions and envelops the struggling souls, eternal fragments of the Supreme. They must free themselves from this material tree and seek the Supreme Person, who dwells in the hearts of all, to enter the realm of everlasting light.

3   *The form of this tree is not visible to those in this world. They do not know where it ends, where it begins, or where its foundation is. But with the strong weapon of detachment one must cut down this deep-rooted tree.*

4   *Thereafter, seek the place from which one never returns, and there surrender to the original Supreme Person from whom all this has extended since time immemorial.*

The complex web of the material world is symbolized by the World Tree. The tree is upside down because it is rooted in the highest reality and extends down into the world of shadows. It is a reflection of the real tree of the spiritual world, like the illusory tree reflected upside down in the water along the bank of a river.

Leaves give shade, and the leaves of this tree are the sacred writings that give relief to those who shelter beneath them. A banyan tree grows secondary roots that hang down from its branches; similarly this tree has secondary roots bound to human actions. Our actions while living as humans on earth create karmic reactions that shape our future lifetimes in other parts of the tree. These karmic roots are deep and bind us to further existence within the tree.

So long as we are attached to the World Tree we will continue wandering from branch to branch, not knowing where it begins or ends. But if we give up our attachment, following Krishna's repeated advice throughout the *Gita*— neither clinging to the tree nor pushing it away—it will cease to bind us and we will be able to cut down its illusory form.

THE LUMINOUS WORLD

5   *That everlasting place is reached by the wise who are free from pride, illusion, and false attachments, ever devoted to the spirit, finished with material desires, and freed from the dualities of happiness and distress.*

6   *That place is not illuminated by the sun, or moon, or fire. Those who go there never return—that is my supreme abode.*

The eternal world is self-luminous and has no need of light. In contrast this world is dark. When our sun sets, our world reverts to shadows, and in the deep recesses of space where

THE WORLD TREE

The Blessed Lord said:

1   *It is said there is an eternal banyan tree that has its roots above and its branches below, whose leaves are the sacred hymns. One who knows this tree understands the sacred wisdom.*

2   *The tree's branches extend upward and downward, nourished by the qualities of nature, and their shoots are the pleasures of the senses. Its roots also go downward, bound to the actions of the human world.*

the light of the sun never reaches, permanent darkness reigns. Therefore this world is called the world of darkness. Yet we are creatures of the sun, naturally attracted to light. Similarly, though in this world all beings must die, we are creatures of life who resist the very idea of death. These are some of the clues pointing to another level of reality to which we really belong. That reality is described by Krishna when he describes his home as a place whose natural state is light.

Krishna's home is called *Goloka Vrindavan*. It is described in sacred Hindu literatures as a place made of spirit where everything is full of bliss. In a forest of desire trees he herds white cows and plays games of laughter and love with his childhood friends. Krishna's form is childlike because he and his friends exist beyond time and never age. Although Krishna never leaves Goloka he is present everywhere by his dazzling effulgence, which pervades and supports all beings and all the worlds.

THE SOUL'S JOURNEY THROUGH THE WORLD

7   *The souls in this world are eternal particles of myself, struggling to carry the material mind and senses.*

8   *Leaving one body and entering another, they carry the mind and senses with them as the wind carries the fragrance of a flower.*

9   *Thus ruling over the ears, eyes, tongue, nose, and sense of touch, all centered about the mind, the soul enjoys the pleasures of this world.*

10   *Those who are deluded do not understand how a soul enjoys life in the body under the spell of nature and then departs—but with the eye of knowledge this can be seen.*

11   *Those who strive on the path of yoga see the self within, but those who do not develop self-understanding, however they try, see nothing.*

As particles of God each of us has a small part of his potencies. Wishing to play as gods, we enter this world and attract to ourselves an aura of material energy, made of mind and senses, that gives subtle shape to our desires. This subtle shape, when clothed in a physical body, reveals the underlying beauty of the soul in a material form through which the soul can manipulate and enjoy matter. We can understand from Krishna's description that the physical

senses of a particular body are extensions of the subtle senses that the soul carries from one body to another. Similarly, those subtle senses are themselves emanations of the eternal spiritual senses of the soul.

Being only a very small fragment of God, in enjoying the world the soul comes under the spell of God's deluding energy, called *maya*. Forgetting our eternal spiritual identity, we are bewildered into accepting the covering of mind and senses as our true self.

Deep down, however, as we travel from one body to another, we retain the memory of our true selves, and with it the knowledge of our loving relationship with the Supreme Lord. This memory haunts us, and inspires us to search for perfect love in this world. As eternal beings we cannot bear the repeated experience of death, or having to part from those we love, and in our pursuit of love and happiness we suffer the pains and misfortunes of this imperfect existence. Sometimes in this frustrated state we hear the voice of the Supersoul, reminding us from within of our spiritual nature, or we hear from the sources of sacred wisdom, or from the mouths of realized souls. Then spiritual knowledge arises in our hearts and we awaken on the path of spiritual self-development.

ABOVE KRISHNA'S FORM APPEARS CHILDLIKE BECAUSE HE NEVER AGES.

CHAPTER 15

THE SUPREME PERSON

12 *The splendor of the sun, illuminating this world and reflected in the light of the moon and the glow of fire—that splendor is mine.*

13 *I enter the earth, holding her in space and sustaining all creatures. I become the moon, giving flavor and nourishment to all plants.*

14 *I dwell in all living bodies as the fire of digestion, and with the vital airs digest all kinds of foods.*

15 *I am seated in everyone's heart. From me come remembrance, knowledge, and forgetfulness. All sacred books lead to me, their knower and their creator.*

16 *There are two kinds of persons in this world, the transient and the eternal. Created beings are transient, but when they are united with the Supreme they are eternal.*

17 *Besides these is the highest person called the Supersoul, the eternal God who enters this world and maintains it.*

18 *I am beyond the transient and above even the eternal; therefore I am celebrated in the world and in the Vedas as that Supreme Person.*

19 *Those who know me without doubt as the Supreme Person know everything, and absorb themselves wholly in my service, Arjuna.*

20 *I have now disclosed to you this most secret teaching, sinless one. Understanding this you are enlightened, and all your endeavors are made perfect.*

The voice of Krishna directs us to worship the Supreme Lord as the One without a second—the original eternal person who is the source of all other eternal persons. He lives in everything, giving it life and support. How do planets float weightlessly in space, perfectly maintaining their orbits? We take such perfection for granted, but such arrangements

are the work of the Supersoul who keeps all bodies on their courses. If for a moment he ceased his work we would all perish.

While passing from one lifetime to another, the soul forgets the past, and this forgetfulness is also a gift of God. For if we did not forget, how could we continue to live? The pain of separation from those we love is mitigated by passing time to make it possible for us to undertake new ventures and discover new truths. All is known to our subconscious selves, but such knowledge is more than we could bear in the midst of the illusions of material life. We have chosen to forget, in order to experience independence from God, and learn what we must learn. That forgetfulness

LEFT THE COOL LIGHT OF THE MOON COMES FROM KRISHNA.

BELOW KRISHNA IS ALL AROUND US — LIKE THE NECESSITIES OF LIFE THAT WE TAKE FOR GRANTED — WATER, AIR, AND SUNLIGHT.

is a gift of God, and when the time comes for us to remember the truth again, the memory of ourselves and the understanding it brings are also gifts of God.

He is with us all the time, inviting us to give him our love. This is the highest teaching of the *Bhagavad Gita*. The great paradox of life is that the things that are most dear to us turn out to be the things we already have—food, water, air, sunlight, life itself, and the love of those near to us. It is only when we lose these most basic things that we appreciate how good they are.

When the light of the sun is hidden behind the clouds we long to see the sun again, and when its warm light returns to us, our spirits are uplifted. Yet the sun, and every one of nature's blessings, are all manifestations of Krishna. He is with us always, and our greatest blessing is his constant friendship. When we understand this, we will return Krishna's love with our devotion and service in all we do. That spirit of service will make everything clear, and then our lives will be complete.

16

LIGHT AND DARK

Living beings are covered by two natures: divine or demoniac. The demoniac nature creates misery and leads ever downward into darkness. Avoid therefore the doors to darkness—lust, anger, and greed—by heeding the books of wisdom.

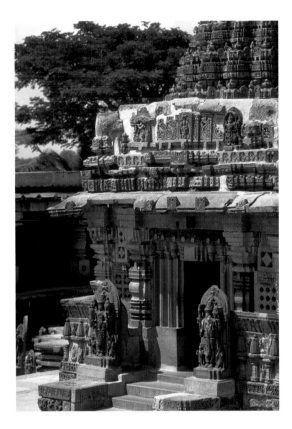

The divine qualities of the soul can be covered by the mantle of the demoniac nature, as illustrated in the story of the gatekeepers of heaven. These two eternal servants of Vishnu chose to enter this world in the garb of demons for three lifetimes. In each life they caused terror and destruction, before being slain by Vishnu and returning to be his eternal servants. Their names are Jaya and Vijaya, and their images often adorn the gateposts of temples of Vishnu, recalling the soul's capacity to choose illusion. Their example teaches that those who seem demoniac are in a temporary condition and will eventually return to Krishna.

We have already learned that forgetfulness is a gift of God. If a soul desires to forget the love of God, even to the extent of wishing to kill him, God covers that soul with a veil of oblivion and gives the soul a birth that will lead to the demoniac nature. Likewise, for those who have chosen to journey toward God, birth to the divine nature leads them on that journey. Most of us experience both tendencies, toward and away from God, and our higher nature must struggle with a darker side. Krishna urges us to choose goodness and light.

Between lives a soul chooses to reenter the world in a particular womb and develop the body and mind that express that soul's desires, with a particular combination of the qualities of nature. Once born we must follow the nature we have chosen, but how we choose to live this present life affects our future destination. Each moment offers us a choice of who we wish to be.

DIVINE AND DEMONIAC NATURES

The Blessed Lord said:

1–3 *These are the qualities that belong to those born to the divine nature: fearlessness, purification of one's existence, cultivation of spiritual knowledge, generosity, self-control, willingness to serve, study of the sacred books, austerity, simplicity, nonviolence, truthfulness, freedom from anger, renunciation, tranquillity, aversion to faultfinding, compassion for all beings, freedom from craving, gentleness, modesty, steady determination, energy, forgiveness, fortitude, cleanliness, and freedom from malice and pride.*

4 *These belong to those born to the demoniac nature: hypocrisy, arrogance, conceit, anger, harshness, and ignorance.*

5 *It is said that the divine nature leads to freedom and the demoniac to bondage. Do not fear, Arjuna, for you were born to the divine nature.*

THE DARK SIDE

6 *Two kinds of beings are created in this world: the divine and the demoniac. The divine have been described at length—now hear about the demoniac.*

7 *The demoniac do not know what is to be done and what is not to be done. No purity, good conduct, or truth are found in them.*

8 *They say this world has no meaning, no cause, and no God, and arises from nothing more than the passionate combination of male and female.*

9 *Holding these misguided views and lost to themselves, they become enemies of the world, flourishing through harmful and destructive works.*

10   *Ruled by insatiable lust, filled with hypocrisy and pride, they are deluded by false ideas and sworn to impure work.*

11   *Convinced that there is nothing higher than the gratification of their desires, they are beset with immeasurable fears that end only with death.*

12   *Bound by a never ending web of desires, absorbed in lust and anger, they amass wealth by dishonest means for the satisfaction of their ambitions.*

The demoniac nature appears from these verses to be a disease of the soul—a delusional state that is based on a denial of all that is good. We have learned from Krishna that the quality of darkness can overwhelm the other two qualities of nature in this world, and it is clear that a soul caught up in the demoniac nature is ruled by this force of darkness and destruction.

A symptom of the state of darkness is surrender to sensual pleasures. Pleasure comes of its own accord as part of a balanced life, but when the mind becomes obsessed with its pursuit and enslaved by it, pleasure turns to pain and obscures the spirit. A person in this condition falls under the power of the senses into the downward spiral, vividly described in the second chapter, that leads to madness and fear. This experience becomes a nightmare from which there is no escape, except by the grace of God.

The powers of darkness are at work wherever the few profit from the misfortune of the many. Today the planet's soil, air, and water are being poisoned by the activities of a minority of people who have grown powerful under the influence of darkness, and careless of the welfare of the planet or its inhabitants. The ambitions of just a few such people of this demoniac tendency can cause a great deal of havoc for everyone else.

BELOW LIGHT AND DARK ARE TWO SIDES OF THE SAME REALITY— THIS WORLD CANNOT BE WITHOUT THEM.

THE MIND OF DARKNESS

13–15 *Deluded by ignorance, the mind of darkness thinks: "I have gained this much today toward achieving my ambitions. This wealth is mine, and more will be mine tomorrow. I have destroyed my enemy and I will destroy others too. I am in control, I enjoy as I please, I am successful, powerful, and happy. I am wealthy and aristocratic and no one is my equal. I shall make sacrifice, give in charity, and celebrate."*

16 *Distracted by countless worries, bound by a network of illusions and addicted to sense enjoyment, the demoniac fall into the depths of darkness.*

17 *Conceited and obstinate, proud and intoxicated with their wealth, they make a show of religion without caring for its true form or meaning.*

18 *Overcome by ego, strength, arrogance, lust, and anger, these envious people hate me in their own bodies and in others.*

19 *Birth after birth, I throw these cruel, hateful, and degraded people into the wombs of the demoniac.*

20 *Born repeatedly among the demoniac and not reaching me, these deluded ones sink ever downward.*

These verses paint a frightening picture of the demoniac mind, which thinks nothing of killing those who get in its way. People with such minds, seeing all competitors as enemies, drag those around them into conflicts, inciting wars and massacres. The root of their disordered and destructive behavior is God-hatred and self-hatred. Their spiritual propensity for love turns to hatred toward God, toward all others, and toward themselves.

Two questions need to be answered here. How can a soul, loving by nature, develop such a hateful condition? And how can a compassionate God throw the deluded soul repeatedly into darkness? If we consider our experience of darkness we will get some idea. When we turn from the sun we see our shadow, for in this world all that is required for darkness to be present is the absence of light. Similarly, when the doors

LEFT THE DOORWAY TO DARKNESS IS OFFERED BY KRISHNA TO THOSE WHO WISH TO FORGET HIM COMPLETELY.

to the soul are firmly closed, an illusory form of darkness appears. This shadow form resembles the self, but has no real substance. It is a negation. We have heard in the fourteenth chapter that the quality of darkness is part of the nature of this world of matter, and that its basic characteristic is ignorance—an absence of understanding. A person in darkness has no conception of right and wrong, and no regard for the guidance of scripture.

The scriptures say that God is neutral toward all beings, and responds to their desires without prejudice. If a soul wishes to forget God utterly, God puts that soul in the state of darkness so the soul will never have to perceive him. However, Krishna does not forget that soul, and by his grace the soul may eventually be woken from oblivion. We are told that Krishna comes to slay those who are completely lost, putting an end to their nightmare. The doors that open on darkness, and close on the soul, can be reopened. These doors are described in the following verses.

THE DOORS TO DARKNESS

21 *Three doors of self-destruction lead to this place of darkness: lust, anger, and greed. Therefore give up these three.*

22 *A person who escapes these three doors of darkness works for self-improvement and then reaches the supreme destination.*

23 *One who behaves whimsically, rejecting the teachings of the scriptures, is unable to achieve perfection, happiness, or the highest goal.*

24 *Therefore be guided in how to live and what to avoid by learning from sacred books, and live in this world by their teachings.*

Having explained the perils of the demoniac nature, Krishna urges us at all costs to avoid the doors that lead to it. Lust, greed, and anger are everywhere evident in a world dominated by the quality of passion, but they are to be neither condemned nor encouraged. Krishna's advice has already been given at the end of the fourteenth chapter that one should be neutral toward them, for aversion is another side of attachment. However, to cultivate the urges of lust, greed, and anger is to open the doors to darkness.

We live in times when the dangers of these doors are not generally understood. The human urges of lust, greed, and anger are encouraged by commercial interests that seek to

ABOVE BE GUIDED IN THIS WORLD BY THE WISDOM OF SACRED BOOKS, AND SO AVOID THE DANGERS OF DARKNESS.

profit from the darker side of human nature. The proliferation of loveless sex, intoxication, harmful technology, and weapons of destruction is part of the result. A more profound effect of opening these doors to darkness is that the doors of the soul are closed. In a world of hardships this is the greatest cruelty, for it takes from people their vision and hope. The greatest love one can show others is to help them reawaken their divine nature, bringing to their lives a vision of truth, hope, and joy.

The teachings of all the world's religions agree that lust, greed, and anger must be overcome if we wish to have peace. To help us understand this spiritual psychology, for our individual welfare and the future welfare of human society, Krishna describes in detail the symptoms of the qualities of nature in the remaining two chapters.

17

THREE KINDS OF FAITH

Faith is essential to all people, and is of three kinds: faith in the divine, faith in the powers of this world, and faith in spirits. According to their natures, people have different faiths, eat different foods, and sacrifice for different causes, but without faith they achieve nothing.

THREE FAITHS

Arjuna said:

1   *Krishna, what of those who worship with faith but do not follow the guidance of scripture? Are they in goodness, passion, or darkness?*

The Blessed Lord said:

2   *Souls in this world develop faith of three kinds according to their natures—in goodness, passion, or darkness. Now hear about these.*

3   *One's faith expresses one's own nature. A person is made of faith and faith makes a person.*

4   *Those in goodness worship the gods, those in passion worship demons and powerful beings, and those in darkness worship ghosts and the spirits of the departed.*

5–6   *Apart from these are those who, driven by lust and attachment, full of hypocrisy and pride, undergo harsh penances not recommended in the scriptures. They senselessly torture their bodies as well as me within them. Their intentions are demoniac.*

People see what they believe, rather than believe what they see—this is the power of faith. The nature people are born with, influenced by their subsequent experiences, leads them to their individual faith. Persuasion and argument cannot change people's faith unless they are willing to change: as it is said, "One persuaded against his will is of the same opinion still." A person's faith develops and changes through experience, prayer, and by association with people of faith.

Three classes of faithful person are recognized by Krishna. As already assured in the seventh chapter, Krishna helps all these, strengthening their faith and giving them the results to which they aspire. But those last described above, who senselessly torture their bodies, have faith in no one and consequently gain nothing except darkness.

LEFT RELIGIOUS SACRIFICES REWARD MATERIAL DESIRES—OR FOR THOSE WHO DESIRE NO REWARD—BRING THE HAPPINESS OF GOODNESS.

Throughout this section of the *Bhagavad Gita* classifications are made of the inclinations and behavior of people under the different qualities of nature. We should understand these as archetypes, rather than distinct groups of people. Each of us has our individual nature, which is made up of all three qualities. The classifications given here are guidance to help us understand our natures and the consequences of our actions, and to make good choices in life.

THREE FOODS

7   *People are attracted to three kinds of food, sacrifice, penance, and giving. Now hear their classifications.*

8   *Foods that are tasty, wholesome, and satisfying, that give long life, vitality, strength, health, happiness, and satisfaction, are liked by those in goodness.*

9   *Foods that are excessively bitter, sour, salty, hot, acidic, or dry, causing discomfort, misery, and disease, are liked by those in passion.*

10   *Foods not freshly cooked, tasteless, decomposed, or stale, consisting of leftovers and impure things, are liked by those in darkness.*

Our choice of food affects our state of health in body, mind, and spirit. The system of Ayurvedic medicine recommends the appropriate food for the health of the body according to our physical type. For peace of mind and good *karma* one should eat vegetarian foods, causing less violence and taking less of the planet's resources. And for spiritual well-being, food cooked with love and devotion is beneficial, since consciousness goes into cooking. Best of all is food offered to Krishna.

THREE KINDS OF SACRIFICE

11   *Sacrifice made according to scripture, as a matter of duty, with no desire for reward, is in goodness.*

12   *Sacrifice made for the sake of a reward, or out of pride, is in passion.*

13   *Sacrifice that is faithless, with no regard for scripture, prayers, or the religious, in which no food is distributed, is in darkness.*

ABOVE DEPENDING ON THEIR INDIVIDUAL NATURE, DIFFERENT PEOPLE LIKE DIFFERENT KINDS OF FOOD.

The intention of the worshiper matters more than the outward form of a sacrifice or a religious ritual. Most worship in human society is performed for the sake of material reward or security. Since God is the father of all, it is natural to ask him for material benefits—such as praying for daily bread—and religion certainly brings prosperity and many blessings. But the true result of religion is to bring an end to the cycle of birth and death. This comes only to those who sacrifice without attachment, out of duty or love.

THREE PENANCES

14   *Penance of the body is to serve God, the devout, the teacher, and superiors, and to be clean, simple, chaste, and nonviolent.*

15   *Penance of the voice is to speak to what is truthful, pleasing, edifying, and gentle, and to recite the scriptures.*

16   *Penance of the mind is peacefulness, simplicity, silence, self-control, and purity of heart.*

17   *This threefold penance, performed with great faith by those devoted to the Supreme and not desiring material rewards, is called penance in goodness.*

18   *Penance done for the sake of show, to earn respect, honor, and worship, that is unsteady and does not last, is in passion.*

19   *That misguided penance that tortures the self, seeking to harm others, is in darkness.*

It is said that human life is meant for penance. The penances recommended here, of body, words, and mind, including service to our parents and teachers, bring illumination and happiness. A life without penance, however, with no sense of sacrifice for a higher cause, will not bring satisfaction. Extreme penance that hurts the body and mind—for example, prolonged fasting—gives pain to God and is not recommended for any purpose.

THREE KINDS OF CHARITY

20   *Charity given selflessly to a worthy person at the right time and place is in goodness.*

21   *Charity given grudgingly to gain some advantage is in passion.*

22   *Charity given to unworthy people, at an improper place and time, without care or respect, is in darkness.*

There are many opportunities in life to give to those who need help. Such chances bestow benefit upon the giver as well as the receiver. Therefore those who ask for help are a blessing to the rest of us. But as with sacrifice and penance,

RIGHT IF WE CAN FIND TRUTH AND GOODNESS EVEN WHERE IT IS HARD TO SEE, WE WILL FIND GOD IN ALL THE WORLD AND BE HAPPY.

the motivation is important. If we give selflessly our love will increase. And if we give selflessly, while remembering the Supreme, we will be released from material life. The greatest gift we can give to others is knowledge of the self and of God, for that is the key to ending all suffering.

OM TAT SAT

23   *Om Tat Sat—these three words represent Absolute Truth. They were used to consecrate priests, scriptures, and sacrifices.*

24   *Those who follow the* Vedas *therefore always begin their sacrifice, penance, and charity by chanting Om.*

25   *Those who seek liberation, not desiring personal reward, make sacrifice, penance, or charity while chanting Tat.*

26   *To represent truth and goodness, and on any auspicious occasion, chant Sat.*

27   *Sat denotes dedication to sacrifice, penance, and charity and anything done with such intentions.*

28   *Sacrifice, penance, or charity practiced without faith are called* asat, *and are of no consequence in this life or the next.*

The mantra *Om Tat Sat* invokes the presence of the Supreme Lord at all times and places. By chanting this mantra, or the *Hare Krishna* mahamantra, or any transcendental mantra containing the names of God, all of life can be sanctified.

Faith of some kind, even if it is not transcendental faith, is needed. Faith requires an openness to trusting others and looking for the good in them. At this point in the *Gita*, having heard how to discriminate between the apparent good and bad in this world, we can do well to remember that it is easy to see the faults in others, but it takes some effort to find their good qualities. The faults we see elsewhere usually reflect our own faults, for it is easier to see them in others than to admit them in ourselves. However, in either case the faults we see are not to be hated, but are to be recognized and learned from.

On the spiritual path we develop different ways of seeing the world. The beginner sees God in the place of worship, in the standard religious practices, and in the scriptures. Next we perceive the presence of God more widely: in the Supreme Lord, in his devotees, in the innocent, and in those who hate God. One who sees these four relates differently to each: surrendering to God, serving his devotees, befriending the innocent, and avoiding the hateful. A further level of perception may be given by God's grace: to see God present everywhere and all beings as his servants. A person with this vision makes no distinction between the divine and the demoniac, seeing past all external coverings to recognize the soul within, and the Supersoul in all.

These three ways of spiritual vision of the world each occur naturally in the life of a devotee of God. Beginning with the faithful worship of the Lord, and learning from others who have faith, we can discover truth and goodness even where it is hard to see. In this way we will find God in all the world and be happy.

18

THE FINAL MESSAGE

Goodness, passion, and darkness color all forms of work, and happiness. Yet all occupations, however imperfect, can find perfection in the service of God. "Abandon other paths and just remember me," concludes Krishna. "I will release you from all fear."

RENOUNCING THE RESULTS OF WORK

Arjuna said:

1   *Dear Krishna, I want to understand the nature
of detachment and renunciation.*

The Blessed Lord said:

2   *Renunciation is giving up work that is selfish, and
detachment is giving up the results of work. So say
the learned.*

3   *Some consider all work should be given up as
flawed, whereas others say works of sacrifice, charity,
and penance should never be given up.*

4   *Listen to my conclusion about detachment,
which is said to be of three kinds.*

5   *Works of sacrifice, charity, and penance should
never be given up, for they purify even the wise.*

6   *But such work should be done without wishing
to enjoy the results. This is my firm opinion.*

7   *Religious obligations should not be given up. Such
misguided renunciation is said to be in darkness.*

8   *To give up work as troublesome, so as to avoid
discomfort, brings no merit and is renunciation
in passion.*

9   *To work as a matter of duty, without attachment for
results, is renunciation in goodness.*

10   *The wise renouncer of the world, full of goodness and
free of doubts, neither avoids unpleasant work, nor
seeks pleasant work.*

11   *A soul living in this world cannot entirely give up
work. But one who gives up the results of work is
truly renounced.*

12   *Those who desire to enjoy the results of their
actions will receive those results after death—
pleasant, unpleasant, and mixed. Not so the
one who is detached.*

No one likes being forced to work, but in this world we
cannot renounce work, because we must work to survive.
Work, however, is about far more than simple survival or
earning material wealth. From the standpoint of the *Gita*
we learn that work offers the path to freedom and spiritual
fulfillment. Even those whose work is not of their own
choosing can find satisfaction by working in a spirit of
detachment. We must understand the difference between
immediate and long-term benefit. Pleasant work may bring
immediate satisfaction, but work as a sacrifice brings long-
term happiness. In any case, the one who works without
attachment for reward receives the greatest benefit of work,
namely spiritual freedom. The way to cultivate this spirit of
detachment is to remember that the self, as spirit separate
from the body and mind, is not the direct cause of work, as
will be made clear by Krishna in the following verses.

FIVE CAUSES OF ACTION

13   *Learn from me the five causes for the success of any
action, as they are taught in scripture.*

14   *The place of action, the actor, the senses,
the endeavor, and ultimately the Divine:*

15   *These five are the causes of whatever is done,
right or wrong, with body, words, or mind.*

16   *One who sees only the self as actor sees imperfectly
and without intelligence.*

17   *Even one who slays all these people—if acting
without ego and with clear intelligence—slays no one
and is not bound.*

We may think that we are alone in doing all our work, but
although it is we who supply the desire, our desire is
fulfilled for us with the help of the other four causes
mentioned here, namely the place of action, which is the
body, the senses and organs of the body that supply the
endeavor, the vital energies that flow within the body, and
ultimately the divine sanction of the Supersoul. We cannot
understand how our heart beats or our digestion functions.
Nor do we know how, when we wish to learn some particular

skill, we are able to do so. Ultimately all this is made possible by the Supersoul who lives within us. If we remain always conscious of the Supersoul, recognizing that without him we can do nothing, all our work will take on a divine dimension. Work in such a spirit cannot bind us. Even Arjuna, fighting as a soldier according to his nature and his duty, remains free from *karma* by working in such a spirit.

131

THREE KINDS OF KNOWLEDGE

18 *Knowledge, the objects of knowledge, and the knower are the three impulses to action. The senses, the work, and the actor are the three ingredients of action.*

19 *Now I will explain to you the three kinds of knowledge, work, and actor, according to the science of the three qualities of nature.*

20 *Knowledge that perceives in all beings one imperishable nature, undivided in the divided, is in goodness.*

21 *Knowledge that perceives in all beings different natures, separate in each, is in passion.*

22 *But that which takes one form as if it were all, not founded on any truth, is meager and said to be in darkness.*

Those who are enlightened by goodness see the underlying unity of all beings because of their shared inner nature, and honor the same spirit present in animals and plants as in humans. Those influenced by passion pay more attention to outer differences, and encourage party spirit and rivalry. Darkness blinds us to anything except outer form, and is insensitive to the varieties of nature that distinguish one being from another.

ABOVE ENLIGHTENED BY GOODNESS, WE CAN SEE THE SAME SPIRIT PRESENT IN ANIMALS AND PLANTS AS IN HUMANS.

THREE KINDS OF WORK AND THREE ACTORS

23 *Work done in the course of duty, without like or dislike, and with no desire to enjoy any result, is said to be in goodness.*

24 *Work done egotistically to satisfy selfish desires and with great effort, is said to be in passion.*

25 *Work done in illusion, without care for consequences, loss, or pain, or for one's own capacity, is said to be in darkness.*

26 *The actor without selfish attachment or ego, steadfast and determined, unwavering in success or failure, is said to be in goodness.*

27 *The actor who is full of desire and motivated by results, who is greedy, aggressive, and impure, easily moved to elation or depression, is said to be in passion.*

28 *The actor who is undisciplined, vain, obstinate, deceitful, rude, lazy, morose, and procrastinating is said to be in darkness.*

The person influenced by goodness disregards the superficial likes and dislikes of the mind, preferring to know that a task is worth doing as a matter of duty. It is better to see an action in terms of its consequences, understanding clearly why it should be done, than be ruled by the whims of the mind. If we train ourselves to learn the consequences of our acts by observation and by learning from the teachings of sacred writings, it will be easier for us to accept the right course of action.

THREE KINDS OF UNDERSTANDING AND WILL

29   *Now hear from me in detail of the different kinds of understanding and will, according to the three qualities of nature.*

30   *Understanding of when to act or not act, what to do or avoid doing, what is harmful or safe, and what binds or gives freedom, is in goodness.*

31   *Understanding that cannot distinguish right from wrong, or what to do from what to avoid doing, is in passion.*

32   *Understanding clouded by illusion, that thinks wrong to be right, and sees everything backward, is in darkness.*

33   *Will made unfailing by yoga practice, that holds firmly the mind, senses, and life energy, is in goodness.*

34   *Will that clings to duty, wealth, and pleasure, desiring their fruits, is in passion.*

35   *The will of a foolish person, preoccupied with dreams, fear, grief, depression, and illusion, is in darkness.*

By the regular practice of yoga one's mind becomes steady, and one's heart is opened to the inner peace of the soul. This makes one self-sufficient, not dependent for happiness on external stimulus for the mind and senses. In such a state it is easier to hear and understand the wisdom of scripture, and to have it confirmed from within by the voice of the Supersoul. Then it is possible to understand what to do or not to do, and to be steady in one's actions and convictions.

BELOW THE DIVERSE WEB OF HUMAN ACTIONS AND RELATIONSHIPS IS WOVEN FROM GOODNESS, PASSION, AND DARKNESS.

THREE KINDS OF HAPPINESS

36   *Now hear from me of the three kinds of happiness whose repeated enjoyment eventually brings an end to distress.*

37   *Happiness arising from the calm of self-understanding, that seems like poison at the beginning but turns to nectar at the end, is said to be in goodness.*

38   *Happiness based on the pleasures of the senses, that seems like nectar at the beginning but turns to poison at the end, is said to be in passion.*

39   *Happiness arising from sleep, laziness, and forgetfulness, that is self-delusion from beginning to end, is said to be in darkness.*

40   *No being, on earth or among the gods in heaven, is free of the influence of the three qualities of goodness, passion, or darkness.*

Living beings must have happiness, but the happiness of this world cannot satisfy the soul—it is like a drop of water in the desert: enough to make us want more but not enough to satisfy. This world is not a happy place because all who are born must experience disease, old age, and finally death. Yet in the midst of pain the heart continues to hope for happiness because our spirit is *ananda*—"joyful."

The best kind of happiness, therefore, is the kind that may begin with hardship, but grows steadily with time. This is the happiness of goodness. If we follow the principles of the *Bhagavad Gita* we can taste this happiness.

The happiness of passion ends in disappointment because it is based on the temporary pleasures of the senses. When the body is young it is attractive and everyone wants to see and touch it, but as the body ages, it loses its appeal. In old age we mourn the lost pleasures of youth. Although we will be offered the chance to be reborn and taste again those pleasures, we will also have to experience again their loss and the pain of old age. This disappointment will be repeated until we learn to look within, and to Krishna, for happiness.

The rewards of passion soon pall, and if the soul will not turn to Krishna, disillusion turns the soul toward darkness and forgetfulness, and to the oblivion of sleep and intoxication. However, the possibility of awakening to the spiritual joy of the soul is always present by the grace of Krishna. The joy of the spirit brings happiness beyond all three kinds of material happiness. In the meantime, Krishna urges that we stick to our duties in life, summarized in the following verses, for by these each of us can use our natural good qualities to be gradually elevated, regardless of our present position.

This section completes Krishna's teachings on the three qualities of nature.

THE FOUR OCCUPATIONS

41   *The duties of intellectuals, leaders, merchants, and workers are classed according to their natural qualities.*

42   *Peacefulness, self-control, penance, purity, forgiveness, honesty, knowledge, wisdom, and faith in God—these are the natural duties of intellectuals.*

43   *Courage, strength, determination, resourcefulness, facing the enemy, generosity, and command are the natural duties of leaders.*

44   *Farming, cow protection, and trade are the natural duties of merchants, and service is the natural duty of the workers.*

45   *By following your natural duty, you can achieve perfection. Hear from me how.*

46   *By worshiping with your work the One from whom all beings emanate and by whom all is pervaded, you can achieve perfection.*

47   *The occupation given to you, though imperfect, is better than another's, even perfectly done. Doing your natural duty never brings sin.*

48   *Do not give up your natural work, even if it is faulty, for all undertakings have some fault, as fire is covered by smoke.*

The heart of Krishna's message, given in the tenth chapter, is to absorb ourselves fully in his service, remembering him constantly. But how will an ordinary person, preoccupied with working in this world, accomplish this precious instruction? Here, almost at the end of his teaching, Krishna advises how, by carrying out the work nature has assigned to us, and worshiping the Lord with that work—even though that work may be imperfect—we can achieve perfection.

ABOVE KRISHNA ENCOURAGES EACH OF US TO FOLLOW OUR OCCUPATION, WHATEVER IT MAY BE, AND AT THE SAME TIME TO REMEMBER HIM.

The four occupations Krishna describes here are the four divisions of the Vedic society: *brahmana*, *kshatriya*, *vaishya*, *sudra*. These precise divisions are not recognized in modern society, but they correspond to natural archetypes that are found in all human societies, and so can still act as a general guide for applying the principle of sacred work. This principle is that, having learned our natural inclination and cultivating the good qualities associated with it, we work in that way while thinking of God.

Whatever our work, it is bound to have its shortcomings, particularly in today's disordered world. There are times when our principles must be compromised for the sake of our work, or when our work is compromised by the constraints of the world. Krishna recognizes this and still encourages us. In Arjuna's case, his work is to fight, and Krishna urges him on even though the task in front of him is abhorrent to him, and beset with moral dilemmas. Most of us do not have to face such extreme tests of our faith and determination. Yet each one of us faces tests and difficult choices. If we follow the principles taught by Krishna we will find that we have his support and protection in everything that we do.

ABOVE SOME ARE DRAWN AWAY FROM THE WORLD, WHILE OTHERS REMAIN
WORKING IN THE WORLD—ALL CAN ACHIEVE SURRENDER TO KRISHNA.

SPIRITUAL JOY

49   *One who is intellectually detached, self-controlled,
and without desires can by practice of renunciation
attain perfect freedom from* karma.

50   *Arjuna, learn from me briefly how by achieving
this perfection you also attain* Brahman, *the stage
of highest knowledge.*

51   *With clear intelligence and controlled mind,
disregarding outside sensations such as sound,
putting aside likes and dislikes,*

52   *Living in seclusion, eating little, controlling thought,
word, and deed, absorbed always in meditation,
cultivating detachment,*

53   *Abandoning ego, power, pride, lust, anger,
possessions, with no sense of ownership and
being peaceful—thus you achieve* Brahman.

54   *One absorbed in Brahman is full of spiritual joy and
no longer sorrows or desires. Such a person, being
equal toward all beings, attains pure devotion for me.*

These verses return us to the theme of the sixth chapter by
describing the path of complete renunciation of the world,
in response to Arjuna's question about renunciation at the
beginning of this chapter. A small number of men and
women in all societies are called away from the world to
a life of penance, prayer, and contemplation. Their path
leads them to the *Brahman* consciousness, where they
experience everything as spirit and enjoy spiritual rapture,
free from all anxieties. Those who remain serving Krishna in
the world, and those who contemplate *Brahman* in solitude,
both arrive at the same place: pure devotion for Krishna.
This perfect stage of self-surrender marks the entrance
to eternal life, and brings us to the conclusion of Krishna's
teachings in the *Bhagavad Gita*.

PERFECT DEVOTION

55   *By devotion you come to know all about me, and
in truth who I am. Once you know me truly, you can
enter my abode.*

56   *Though working in all kinds of ways under my
protection, my devotee reaches the eternal
imperishable abode by my grace.*

57   *Mentally surrender all your work to me, making
me the goal of your life. Be absorbed on the path
of devotion, always conscious of me.*

58   *Be conscious of me and by my grace you will
overcome all difficulties. But if through ego you
do not hear me, you will be lost.*

59   *If out of ego you decide not to fight, your resolve
will be in vain, for your nature will make you fight.*

60   *Bound by your natural inclination you will be forced
to do the very thing that in your delusion you resist.*

61   *The Lord dwells in the hearts of all beings, making
them wander under the spell of illusion as if seated
on a machine of maya.*

62   *Surrender to him utterly, Arjuna. By his grace you will
gain ultimate peace and reach the eternal abode.*

63   *Thus I have told you this most secret of all secret
knowledge. Reflect on this fully, and then do as
you wish.*

Krishna takes responsibility for all our wanderings. Even if we should wish to act against our nature, still we could not. Therefore he urges us to resign ourselves fully to him. However, at this final point Krishna leaves a choice. He will not force us to love him — how can he? The choice is ours, and that precious freedom lies at the heart of the *Gita* and the paradox of life. Though we are ruled by the forces that surround us, we are also creatures of free will, and our freedom is honored by the Lord at the cost of everything.

We imagine that we have many choices in life. But in truth our choice is very simple: to serve Krishna with love and understanding, or to be ruled by Krishna's nature. Either way we are servants. We are bound to serve because, though we are eternal spiritual beings, we are very small. By nature we are dominated by the engulfing ocean of Krishna's divine energies. These energies are called maya and can be experienced in two ways. Maya can be understood as Krishna's illusory material nature, which causes us to forget and carries us through the revolving cycle of birth and death. Or maya can be experienced as the embrace of Krishna's everlasting spiritual nature, called *yoga maya*, the loving energy that brings us to him. Our choice is simple: to choose the illusory freedom of forgetfulness, or to choose the embrace of Krishna's love. Within Krishna's existence the individuality of the lover and beloved goes on eternally, and their spiritual exchange of love continually unfolds.

Now everything has been said, and Krishna has only to add his closing words of love and reassurance.

FINAL MESSAGE OF LOVE

64   *Hear once more my final message, the greatest secret of all, spoken for your benefit because you are my dearly beloved.*

65   *Think of me always, become my devotee, worship me and bow down to me. Thus surely you will come to me. I promise you this because you are my dear friend.*

66   *Abandon all kinds of religion and surrender to me alone. I will free you from all sinful reactions. Do not fear.*

RIGHT THE CONSTANT REMEMBRANCE OF KRISHNA — BY CHANTING HIS NAMES — IS CALLED KRISHNA CONSCIOUSNESS.

Krishna repeats the words he spoke at the end of the ninth chapter: "Think of me always." This constant remembrance of Krishna is called Krishna consciousness — to live our life so as always to remember the beautiful cowherd boy who plays his flute in the forests of Vrindavan. Only this time he repeats these words as a promise of friendship. At last it comes down to this. Krishna is our friend who loves us and will save us from anything — we have only to turn to him and accept his love and freely give our love in response. It is the easiest and yet the hardest thing to do: to accept another's love and to give our love in return.

When all has been said in all the teachings of all the religions of the world, only two things remain: the fear of God and the love of God. Krishna consciousness is to bring us from fear to love. Choose love and all fear is gone. This is Krishna's final message.

KRISHNA'S BLESSING

67 *This final secret must not be spoken to one who is not austere, not a devotee, does not wish to listen, or speaks ill of me.*

68 *One who teaches this supreme secret to my devotees offers me the greatest love, and without doubt comes to me.*

69 *No one is dearer to me than such a person, nor on earth will there ever be one more dear.*

70 *I declare that whoever studies this sacred dialogue of ours worships me with the intellect.*

71 *And whoever hears and listens with faith and open heart is liberated and reaches the blessed realms of the virtuous.*

72 *Dear Arjuna, have you heard with attentive mind? Are your ignorance and confusion now dispelled?*

Krishna has already told Arjuna to make his own choice. Now he encourages all those who in the future will study his words to do the same. Reflect deeply on this dialogue, he says, consider it from all angles, and then reach your own conclusion. The *Bhagavad Gita* is not a book of doctrine that must be accepted without question. It is to be studied and reflected upon. If we choose to put faith in Krishna, and apply his instructions in our lives, we will see for ourselves the results of heeding his words of love.

In case we should think that the love spoken of is exclusively between ourselves and Krishna, we are reminded here that all of us are bound together in this ocean of love. The perfect expression of our loving nature is to share the awareness of Krishna's love with all his separated parts who live in this world forgetting him. This will fulfill our natural desire to love others, and open us to receive their love in return. The guru Srila Prabhupada did just this. He chose to share his own love for Krishna by traveling and preaching throughout the world, and writing many books about Krishna. He wrote, "If we learn how to love Krishna, then it is very easy to immediately and simultaneously love every living being."

CONCLUDING WORDS

Arjuna said:

73 *My illusion is destroyed and my memory restored by your grace, Krishna. Free from doubt, I stand ready to follow your instructions.*

Sanjaya said:

74 *Thus I have heard this wonderful dialogue between Krishna and the great-souled Arjuna, which makes my hair tingle.*

75 *By the grace of my guru, Vyasa, I have heard these supreme secrets of yoga directly from the Lord of yoga, Krishna.*

76 *O King, as I remember over and over these sublime and sacred words between Krishna and Arjuna, I am thrilled with joy again and again.*

77 *As I remember time after time Krishna's wonderful form, amazement and joy fill my heart more and more.*

78 *Where there is Krishna, Lord of yoga, and the archer Arjuna, there will surely be fortune, victory, happiness, and morality.*

Sanjaya heard Krishna's words by the grace of his guru, Vyasa, who is credited as the author of the *Mahabharata* and the *Bhagavad Gita*. A guru is one who points the way to Krishna, and it is said that without the grace of such a soul who has seen the truth, no one can find their own way home.

One who chooses to surrender to Krishna is advised to search for a spiritual teacher who is a devotee of Krishna, and to practice *bhakti* yoga, devotional service, under the teacher's guidance. This act of submission opens the door of the heart to receive the blessings of the Lord. If you are unable to find such a teacher, Krishna himself will help you from within.

You only have to chant Krishna's names to fulfill all the teachings of the *Bhagavad Gita*:
Hare Krishna Hare Krishna
Krishna Krishna Hare Hare
Hare Rama Hare Rama
Rama Rama Hare Hare.

GLOSSARY OF KEY CONCEPTS IN THE *BHAGAVAD GITA*

ahamkara	(*aham* "I," *kara* "act") illusory sense of self as being the body or the mind
akarma	inaction: action without karmic reaction (opp. *karma*)
apara	lower, belonging to the lower nature (opp. *para*)
asat	untruth; unreality (opp. *sat*)
asura	person who disobeys dharma, and does harm to others or to the self (opp. *sura*)
atma	self: body, mind, or soul; or the Supreme Spirit (see *jivatma* and *paramatma*)
avatara	one who descends: an appearance of the divine in this world
avidya	ignorance; lack of knowledge (opp. *vidya*)
avyakta	unmanifest, formless, imperceptible; the impersonal aspect of the Supreme; the formless uncreated state of the dormant material energy prior to or in between creations
bhagavan	Supreme Lord, possessor of opulence
bhakta	one who is devoted to the Supreme
bhakti	devotion to the Supreme
bhakti yoga	the path of devotional service to the Supreme
Brahma	the first created being, grandfather of the universe, member of the supposed Hindu trinity
brahma-nirvana	see *nirvana*
brahman	the spiritual nature; the pervasive presence of the Supreme; the Supreme
buddhi	understanding; inspired wisdom
buddhi yoga	the path of constant remembrance of the Supreme
deva	divine being; higher order of created being
dharma	universal religious principles; essential quality that unites all beings with the universe and with God
guna	one of the three primary qualities of nature: *sattva guna*, goodness and illumination; *rajo guna*, passion and creativity; *tamo guna*, darkness and ignorance
isvara	God, the Supreme Controller
japa	soft or silent repetition of a mantra as prayer or meditation, may be counted on a *japa-mala*, string of prayer beads
jivatma	the individual soul
jnana	knowledge
jnana yoga	path of knowledge of the Supreme
jnani	one who practices *jnana*-yoga
karma	action; past actions that accrue results; hence can mean the results of past actions
karma yoga	the path of dedicating actions to the Supreme, thus gaining liberation from the results of action
karmi	one who practices *karma*-yoga
mantra	(*man* "mind," *tra* "release") spiritual sound vibration upon which to focus the mind and senses
maya	"that which is not," or illusion; the creative energy of God that gives rise to illusion
moksha	see *mukti*

mukti	salvation; liberation from the ties of karma and the cycle of rebirth
nirvana	cessation of material existence; the *Bhagavad Gita* uses the term *brahma-nirvana* to indicate that after the false self is extinguished, the true self, *brahman*, remains
para	higher; belonging to the higher nature
paramatma	Supreme Self, or Supersoul, who dwells within every living being
parampara	system of disciplic succession, or lineage of spiritual teaching
prakriti	material nature, the primordial energy of God from which the world is formed
prana	breath; vital force
purusa	Supreme Person; sometimes can mean the individual soul
rajas	the material quality of passion and creativity (see *guna*)
sadhu	saintly person
samadhi	mystical trance; complete absorption in the Supreme
samsara	the seemingly endless cycle of birth, old age, disease, and death
sankhya	one of the six Vedic philosophical systems, *sankhya* analyzes matter into 24 elements with the aim of distinguishing the soul from these 24
sannyasa	complete renunciation
sannyasi	a member of the homeless order of celibate monks
sastra	Vedic literatures; authoritative religious text (see *smriti* and *sruti*)
sat	truth; reality

sattva	the material quality of goodness and illumination (see *guna*)
smriti	remembered; scriptures such as the *Puranas*, based upon discussion of the sruti (see *sruti*)
sraddha	faith in God
sruti	directly heard; revealed scriptures: the Vedic hymns and *Upanishads* (see *smriti*)
sura	godly person, who abides by *dharma*
tamas	the material quality of darkness and ignorance (see *guna*)
tapa	austerity and penance by exercising control of one's own senses
tyaga	renunciation of the results of actions
veda	spiritual knowledge; the ancient Sanskrit hymns directly revealed by God: *Rik Veda*, *Sama Veda*, *Yajur Veda*, and *Atharva Veda*
vidya	cultivation of knowledge; education
visvarupa	universal form of God, as pervading the whole universe
yajna	sacrifice; offering to God as form of worship
yoga	link or union, usually describes the relationship between the soul and God; a spiritual discipline seeking closer union with God; yoga is one of the six Vedic philosophical systems
yogi	one who practices yoga
yuga	cosmic passage of time: the four *yugas* together make a cosmic cycle lasting 4.5 million years, and a thousand such cycles make a cosmic day. The present, fourth, yuga is *Kali Yuga*, a period of disorder and diminishing wisdom and life-span

PICTURE ACKNOWLEDGMENTS

Robyn Beeche: p. 49

CORBIS: pp. 1 Jack Fields, 10 Lindsay Hebberd, 12 Chris Hellier, 14 David Cummings/Eye Ubiquitous,15 Arne Hodalic, 16 Lindsay Hebberd, 18 Jeremy Horner, 19 Tiziana & Gianni Baldizzone, 21 David Cummings/Eye Ubiquitous, 23 Adam Woolfitt, 25 Robert Holmes, 26 Arvid Garg, 28 David Samuel Robbins, 30 Arvid Garg, 31 Earl & Nazima Kowall, 32 Arne Hodalic, 36 Lindsay Hebberd, 38 Ric Ergenbright, 39 Adam Woolfitt, 41 Lindsay Hebberd, 42 Jack Fields, 43 Bob Gibbons/Eye Ubiquitous, 44 Craig Lovell, 50 Chris Lisle, 54 Arne Hodalic, 56 Michael Boys, 58 Bob Krist, 60 Wolfgang Kaehler, 61 David Samuel Robbins, 62 Bojan Brecelj, 64 Michael Freeman, 66 Lindsay Hebberd, 69 Brian A Vikander, 70 David Samuel Robbins, 72 Sheldan Collins, 75 Lindsay Hebberd, 80 Robert Maass, 82 John Noble, 83 Sheldan Collins, 84 Michael Freeman, 86 Stocktrek, 89 David Samuel Robbins, 92 Jerremy Horner, 94 David H.Wells, 95 Jeremy Horner, 96 David Turnley, 97 Brian A Vikander, 98 Jeremy Horner, 100 Lindsay Hebberd, 103 Bojan Brecelj, 112 Lindsay Hebberd, 114 Brian A Vikander, 116 Janez Skok, 118 Sheldan Collins, 120 Lindsay Hebberd, 121 Janez Skok, 122 + 124 + 128 Lindsay Hebberd, 132 Arvid Garg, 133 Jeremy Horner, 135 Lindsay Hebberd, 136 Daniel Laine, 137 Lindsay Hebberd

GETTY IMAGES/The Image Bank: p.78

HUTCHISON PICTURE LIBRARY: pp. 2 John Hatt, 4 + 6 Michael Macintyre, 22 David Brinicombe, 24 John Hatt, 27 Michael Macintyre, 33 Maurice Harvey, 35 Patrico Goycoolea, 46 R.Shaw, 47 Jeremy Horner, 53 Chris Oldroyd, 67 Carlos Friere, 68 Christine Pemberton, 104 Michael Jellife, 106 Patricio Goycoolea, 107 Victor Lamont, 109 Patricio Goycoolea, 110 R.Shaw, 115 Jeremy Horner, 125 Liba Taylor, 127 Jeremy Horner, 131 Maurice Harvey

© B.G. Sharma courtesy of Mandala Press: pp. 7, 74, 90, 113